ONE LAD

A personal account of one sailor's experience of World War II and the D-Day landings

by Frederick Nutt

edited by Hazel Wilkinson

TheWordWorks

Published by The**WordWorks**
84 Holmley Lane
Dronfield
S18 2HS

01246 417737

for St Luke's Hospice, Little Common Lane
Sheffield S11 9NE

A forget-me-not publication

ISBN 0-9549457-0-0
Print and cover design by Sheffield Hallam University

Contents

Acknowledgements

I must pay tribute to Elaine Bird, the staff nurse at St Luke's Hospice who first persuaded me to write this book, and Hazel Wilkinson, my editor and publisher, without whose practical help and encouragement this project would not even have got off the ground, let alone be finished.

Introduction

In 2002, during a brief stay at St Luke's Hospice, Sheffield, for a period of respite, recuperating from the after-affects of radiotherapy for the treatment of cancer, I was browbeaten, cajoled and finally persuaded to write of my experience of the 1939-1945 war, with the idea that someone will read it, even if only my grandchildren. This is that story.

I have not enjoyed writing certain sections of this book, or found it an easy task, sometimes because of ill-health and sometimes because of the painful memories it evoked.

Throughout, I relied on my personal recollections, so I can only apologise in advance for any inaccuracies which may have crept in, but it was a long time ago after all and I can only plead incipient senility.

I am no hero and don't pretend otherwise. We had a job to do and did it. I hope that, like many others, we did it to the best of our ability. After all, we didn't have much option. I would have liked to have revisited the Normandy beaches in 2004, but alone, and not with a crowd or party who would have been, to some extent, tourists, but my health precluded this.

We all have our own memories, some of which are perhaps best forgotten. Writing this brought back some I had almost buried. One remembers the good times, of which there were many, and the comradeship of a ship's crew living in, what you might say, each other's pockets. The war stole our youth and trying to adapt back into 'civvy street' wasn't easy. I still remember it taking ages to get used to sleeping in a bed again: I missed my hammock. We felt like fishes out of water, no pun intended. The world had moved on and we were left in limbo. We were not always welcomed back as I think we upset the status quo. We had grown up far too quickly and our sense of hard won assurance and inability to accept fools and petty unearned authority did not always go down too well. We didn't want thanks or gratitude but a grain of respect would not have gone amiss. That is why I think the war is best forgotten except, perhaps, for a thought now and then for the very, very many who did not come back.

Fred Nutt
2005

Part One

Civvy Street to matelot

Chapter One

My Beginnings

I was born in Sheffield in 1925 at Handsworth which was, in those days, almost a small village on the outskirts of the city. A fair proportion of workers from that area were employed in farming and coalmining. Miners were called colliers in those days and, although I wouldn't suggest that I was brought up in the same degree of deprivation as they endured, I saw enough of it to appreciate their experiences.

My father was a 'little mester' in the grinding industry and employed several men, hand-picked for their skill, although I don't recall much about his work as he died when I was about ten or eleven of the dreaded grinder's disease, silicosis. I was told that he was the last man in Sheffield to grind on sandstone, and the specialised work that he did had to be sent to be done at Birmingham after his death because there was no one with his skills left in the Sheffield area.

There were six children in our family, consisting of two girls: Marjorie and Freda; two boys: me and Arthur; and two more girls: Beryl and Mavis, all progressing upwards in age by about two years. I have often thought that these names were pretty old-fashioned, even for those days. Take my own name for example. It was common practice then for the first-born son to be called after his father, so I was Frederick Richard. Also, being the first son, and because the doctor, Bruce Pettigrew, was a friend of the family, I became Frederick Richard Bruce, an awful mouthful for a little lad.

My mother's name was Ethel and her maiden name was Wainwright. She was born in Mosborough and became a school teacher at the little village of Halfway. To cover the journey from Mosborough to Halfway, her parents bought her a pony and trap, the horse being put out to graze during the day in the school playground, which was actually a field. Some of the pupils living on outlying farms also came to school on ponies. Truly rural, eh?

Although our family was thought somewhat affluent compared with many, I don't think this was so much so after my father died.

In those days, education was not considered to be as important as it is now. We all went to the local council school where our education culminated in taking 'the scholarship', with the intention of gaining one of the limited places at a grammar school. This I managed to do, and went on to Firth Park Grammar

School (where we were known as the bloodnuts because we wore red jackets and caps), having studied just enough to get me through. The advantage of going to a grammar school was that, if one passed the School Certificate, one was expected to work in an office, with its advantages of paid holidays, payment when off ill, and a superannuation fund to provide a pension on retirement. Manual workers didn't enjoy these privileges, although slowly over the years they became almost universal.

Chapter Two
Early days

In those days, there was little in the way of entertainment. No wireless, no TV, no cinema like that known today. There was, however, the odd visit to the Saturday matinee at The Lyric at Darnall. We were given threepence. Twopence was to get us in, the other penny was for the tram fare there and back, and then we had to walk up all the way into Handsworth, about a half mile, making it quite a trip. Occasionally, four of us lads clubbed together the halfpennies meant for the return trip and bought a packet of five Woodbine cigarettes, smoking them as we walked home. Cigarette smoking, although very much frowned on at that age, was not considered the evil it is now, and cigarettes and tobacco were widely advertised, almost as being good for one's health.

Our gang, with a variable loose membership, often congregated at Four Lane Ends, which was at the cross of the roads down to Catcliffe and Orgreave Colliery. There was a wooden hut there with a drop-down front that used to supply cigarettes and soft drinks, such as Tizer and Dandelion and Burdock, to the colliers coming home from their shift at the pit.

The men would all be in their 'pit muck' (there were no pithead baths then) and some had to walk all the way to their homes in Darnall. We used to beg cigarette cards from those who had just bought cigarettes, and thereby saved up to get a full set. I well remember asking for some from one old man - at least, he seemed old to us - and his reply was a testy, 'No! I'm not larnin' yor to smoke.'

However, despite there being no organised entertainment, there were never enough hours in a day for us. We roamed all over the surrounding districts of Woodhouse Mill, Woodhouse, Catcliffe, Treeton and Swallownest - climbing trees, scrumping apples in season, bird-nesting, and sledging and 'slairing' in winter. We prided ourselves on knowing the names of all the common trees, and wild flowers, which had such names as cow parsley (also called motherdie), Brussels lace, devil's bit, toadflax, giant reedmace (often wrongly called bullrush), and many more. Being Sheffielders, none of us would ever be without a pocket knife, used to cut ash wands which were then peeled in alternate bands and used for sword fighting and slashing at tall wild plants, such as cow parsley, from which we made whistles by making a split down one side of a length of six inches or so and including a joint, which effectively blocked up the hollow tube. By blowing down this, if you had done the job properly, you produced a note a bit like a penny whistle. If we produced three or four of these in various lengths we could, sometimes, by tying them together, have a set of panpipes. Errors made experience. I well remember bringing home a huge bunch of meadowsweet, which had a beautiful smell of honey. This was dutifully placed in a vase in the living room as a present for our mother. It was accepted with, I thought, a wry smile. She knew why, and so did we the next morning, as the whole house stank as though all the tomcats in the neighbourhood had held an orgy in our front room. I wonder how many other people had mistakenly done the same as us.

At school, we played marbles and spun peg tops. These were quite cheap and we usually owned two or three. The usual routine was to cut off the peg on top of the top and replace it with a drawing pin. They were beautifully balanced, much better made than the rubbish produced now, and one could become quite adept at picking them up from off the floor and throwing them down again without interrupting the spin. You could also play a game similar to marbles, knocking your opponent's top over. With girls, it was always skipping, using orange box rope begged from the local greengrocer. This was made from the plaited straw used to tie up the flimsily made boxes that the oranges came in. It had a limited life but there was a constant supply.

I well remember one year when there was a glut of little blood oranges which were selling for one hundred for a shilling (five pence) and all the teachers clubbed together and gave every child at the council school two each. Incidentally, I remember a similar thing happened at the Saturday matinee at The Lyric at Darnall. This only happened once, as the amount of orange peel and partly eaten oranges, which rained down from the balcony onto the hapless children below, needed too much cleaning up afterwards. The surface of the roads around the school consisted of very smooth tarmac and was ideal for roller-skating. There were often up to twenty kids there of an evening. These roller skates were quite cheap. You could get a basic set, even from Woolworth's when everything was 'nothing over sixpence', although I seem to think they were sold split into four parts making the real price two bob. However, a very good pair, from Halford's would cost seven and eleven in our old currency, and new wheels, which cost nine old pence, were worn out regularly during the hectic games of roller skating hockey, a game with very few rules except, perhaps, survival of the fittest. Grazed knees, at least, were very common.

Young lads, then, always wore short trousers, often up to the age of sixteen. We wouldn't have been thankful for being given a pair of long trousers, as this would have meant having to fold them up at night into creases, instead of just throwing them on the floor. Most of the young lads at school wore thin machine-knitted jerseys, often with a matching machine-knitted tie, whilst girls usually wore a dress of sorts, often with a white pinafore over the top. As I recall, several boys wore corduroy knee britches, and at least one I knew, wore clogs. These were very cheap and were standard wear for miners and buffer girls.

We also used to make quite effective bows and arrows, imagining ourselves as Robin Hoods. Bows were made of ash, but for arrows we had to resort to off-cuts of dowelling, after spending the whole of a Saturday afternoon planing down a couple of redundant oak stair carpet rods. For flights we used split goose wing quills, easily available then, and the tip was a boot seg stuck into the tip and bound with copper wire. They were pretty accurate and could be dangerous, as I remember – shooting at our garden shed door, with the arrow piercing right through the timber. A catapult was another tool, made from a selected hazel branch, forked just as we liked, and finished with some quarter inch square elastic, which we had to go all the way to Darnall to buy. These could also be very effective and, armed with one of these and a pocketful of pebbles each, we must have been quite a danger to everyone.

After roller skates came bicycles, and everybody owned a bike of some sort or another. The standard was a drop-handlebar racing bike, not that many of us did any racing, it was just the fashion, as it is now with mountain bikes. They were quite cheap then, especially if one got a second hand machine or one that had been passed down. You could buy a brand new bike for thirty bob from Halford's, although these were a bit infra dig, and were derisorily known as 'Wiggies Gas Pipes'. We could then roam much further, out to Worksop and Retford and all points east, then out into Derbyshire.

There is no doubt that the highlights of our year were the 'Whitsuntide treat' and the Handsworth Fair, more often called the Handsworth Feast. The treat started with a tea in the church hall, featuring sandwiches, Sally Lunns, jellies and the like. Before we left, we were all given an apple and orange and a bag of boiled sweets, and then proceeded across the road, down Church Lane to the church fields, where the rest of the afternoon was taken up with races and all sorts of other events. Surprisingly enough, the prizes were always in money, threepence for first place, twopence for second and a penny for third. It was lovely to go home at the end of the day, tired and dirty, but with what seemed like a pocketful of coins.

Handsworth Feast was a massive affair, which had apparently been going on, some said, for a hundred years or more. It was always held on the Fairground, which I suppose was used for grazing cattle for most of the year. One got to it by a path down by the side of the working men's club. You couldn't miss it as you could hear the noise and music from half a mile away. It had the usual merry-go-round, dodgems, and other attractions, making it far superior to the miserable efforts one sees today, and it was cheaper too, as most of the rides were often a penny to go on. Around the outside were the much more interesting stalls, rifle ranges, coconut shies, boxing booths: 'Stand up to our contestant for two minutes and win five pounds.' Many of the local hefty 'sons of the earth' used to try, but I don't recall anyone walking away with the five pounds. There were snake charmers, headless women and so many other attractions, enough to talk about for weeks after.

Chapter Three
Grammar School

Life at grammar school was different, but not all that much. It was an 'all boys' school, which we probably enjoyed as, at that age, girls were just a necessary encumbrance. There were new subjects to learn, and I suppose we got down to work a bit more seriously. 'School Cert' year in 1939 coincided with the outbreak of war, and things like erecting Anderson shelters. As I was the 'man of the house', albeit a poor one, small maintenance jobs were up to me. I particularly liked electrical jobs and learned quite a bit, as well as what electric shocks felt like.

Culmination of grammar school was passing 'the Cert' and looking about for a job. I fancied working in a draughtsman's office, but it appeared that nobody was interested in taking on a school-leaver, as they knew you were going to be called up in two years' time at eighteen. Out of the blue, I received a letter from the L.M.S railway saying that my name had been passed on to them as a possible suitable applicant, provided I passed their medical and written exams. As there seemed to be nothing else in the offing, I took this up, and started work near the middle of

Sheffield, at the Wicker Station, which is no longer there. There was a standard procedure for all trainee staff, which finished with working in the shipping office, which was actually nothing to do with shipping. The working hours were five in the evening until all the work was finished, which was anytime after eleven at night, and often much later. I already knew several of the lads there, of which there were about twenty. We all, on a rota, worked ten days and then had a day off. It was not much fun going to work on Sundays - and all for twenty-five bob a week. It seemed that the only way out for the next two years at least, was to volunteer for the forces: railway work was a reserved occupation so I knew I couldn't be called up.

I applied to the navy's Fleet Air Arm as a pilot, but after more exams and a medical, was told that my eyesight was not good enough. Somewhat worryingly, I was advised that if I tried the Royal Air Force, I would be good enough for them. I thought that maybe it was a different kettle of fish, landing on an aircraft carrier, as opposed to landing on solid ground. For the air force, however, there was a nine months deferment, which was not much good to me, so I wrote to say that I would just join the navy. More medicals and exams, then I was told that I had been accepted into The Royal Navy Youth Scheme as an officer cadet, and asked when did I want to be called up. As I was not yet eighteen, I said a week after my eighteenth birthday, which was the third of August. This day eventually arrived and I was ordered to report to H.M.S Ganges, which was at Shotley, across the river from Ipswich and I duly set off, with much trepidation, wondering what I had let myself in for.

I cannot emphasise too much that lads of eighteen, at that time, were very 'green' and innocent, not at all streetwise in the way such lads are today. Many had never been outside their home town. The furthest I had been in a train was to Grindleford and, as very few families owned a car, travelling was a thing one read about rather than did.

Although my life experience was somewhat limited, it appeared that my physical growth was not. At sixteen I hadn't been tall, just a freckle-faced lad of medium height with ginger hair done in what was then called a donkey crop, or basin crop. But from the age of sixteen to eighteen I shot up in height to 6'1" and weighed twelve and a half stone. I was naturally agile and athletic, game for any mad escapade, and not one to back away from a scrap. I was, at times, referred to as 'that mad bugger' and earned the nickname of 'Bats Nutt.'

Chapter Four
The Senior Service

One never saw such a motley shower of miserable lads as arrived at HMS Ganges, which, incidentally, was a shore establishment training camp and not a proper ship. Several cried themselves to sleep that night, especially the Londoners, and 'I want me mam' was heard from a number. But from then on, we were too busy to think about such things as home, what with kitting out, swimming, square bashing, rifle practice on the range and learning the elements of seamanship, both theoretical and practical. Swimming before breakfast was compulsory until one had passed the required standard, which involved swimming one and a half lengths and then treading water for a couple of minutes - also, swimming a length fully dressed, which is not at all easy. Most passed, eventually. Those that didn't were not allowed to go to sea. All this was in our birthday suits, for reasons of hygiene, and there was no mixed bathing. It was said that the wrens had the same treatment, but no-one ever proved it. Training culminated in climbing most of the way up the one hundred and fifty foot mast. Although there were nets of sorts underneath, it was rumoured that an average of nine were killed each year falling from the top. The truly foolhardy, of which I was one, climbed even further, up a rope ladder, and then scrawmed up the last twelve foot or so of bare mast to stand on the button, about eighteen inches wide with a lightning conductor on top which you could hold between your knees. I must admit I was trembling when I got safely down, but a bet is a bet and it was a matter of honour, fools that we were.

Although training was hard, I think it was enjoyable and it stood us in good stead. During this time, there were various questionnaires and aptitude tests. One of these was intended to be the basis for my career plans. There was one question, 'What do you want to be in the Navy?' To my mind the obvious answer was 'a sailor' but this seemed a bit naïve, so I put down 'electrical artificer', as I had read about this in a library book recently. The consequence of this was that I was then interviewed by the electrical officer, who wanted to know from where I had got this job title. I explained and was then told that this was a 'regular' navy position, which entailed joining as a boy and progressing, eventually, through to the rank of chief petty officer. There was, however, a wartime equivalent designed for converting civilian qualified electricians to the naval standard and, after further questions, which taxed all my remembrances of School Certificate-level physics (which I had passed at 'credit' level) and the practical knowledge I had gained at home, he judged my expertise sufficient, and I was duly sent off to my shore base at Chatham.

I was then sent to Hitchin in Hertfordshire to live in civilian billets, and travelled by train everyday for training at a Royal Ordnance factory at Letchworth. This entailed an exam at the end of each month. If you passed, you went onto the next month, if you failed, you were out. All this I scraped through and managed for six of the nine months required. That was my lot. After that I didn't even understand the questions, never mind the answers. As I had done reasonably well, I found that my knowledge was not to go to waste, and I was transferred to 'combined operations' for specialised training as the electrician on a 'rocket ship', then a secret weapon to be used for assault landings on enemy beaches.

Fortunately, whilst at Hitchin I was able to use the railway ticket issued to me for the Letchworth to Hitchin journey, to have two or three weekends at home, as the same train went on to Sheffield. By getting off at Woodhouse Mill and climbing over the fence, I could walk home the mile and a half, and was able to use the same ticket more than once.

I was then sent to Troon in Scotland for landing craft training. We were in a huge combined forces camp. It was winter, freezing cold all the time, and I was utterly miserable. Our time was spent learning about tank landing craft and we were at sea most days, out around the Isle of Arran and off Lamlash. The weather was pretty foul, but we got to know what it was like handling wet and freezing mooring lines in a howling wind and against driving rain. We weren't particularly impressed to see that, if you stood at the very back of the tank deck, you could see the whole ship bending and flexing in a rough sea. And we weren't surprised to be told that an attempt to send some tank landing craft across the Atlantic had failed when all the ships had broken up and sunk. Not a very reassuring thought. At the forefront of our minds was the question, 'What the hell have we let ourselves in for?'

Whilst there, we were kitted out with all the army uniform, even complete with tropical kit. I already had the full navy kit, also including tropical kit made up of white duck suits and even including a solar topee. I was, therefore, encumbered with three kit bags full of equipment, and my hammock, so any draft to anywhere was a major job. It was a bit like being Lazarus who, perhaps you will remember, was ordered to 'take up thy bed and walk'. Training completed, we then shipped off to Portsmouth for two weeks training at a torpedo school at HMS Vernon. Apparently I was now to be classed as a 'torpedoman', this being the only naval equivalent to being an electrician. The course was interesting, but not much use as I never saw another torpedo again.

Chapter Five
Combined Operations

After Vernon, I was shipped off again. This time is was to Southampton to join my ship which was designated as L.C.T(R) 363, so called because the early ones were made from converted tank landing craft, decked over and fitted with eleven banks of rocket racks, looking like so many toast racks leaning over pointing forward at an angle and capable of holding 1200 seventy-five pound rockets about five inches in diameter and about four feet long. To say it looked odd is an understatement. Just behind this was a heavy v-shaped steel blast screen, intended to deflect the flames and bits and pieces over the side and behind us when the rockets were fired. It was rumoured that on one of the original rocket ships, due to an error, all the rockets had been fired in one salvo, resulting in the bridge and the upper deck superstructure being blasted off the ship together with all the officers and helmsmen – and anyone else nearby. Standing up from a tower on the bridge was a plastic semi-translucent dome, which housed the rotating radar aerial.

I was now in the Close Support Squadron, comprised of rocket ships, flak ships and gun-boats, all made from converted tank landing craft. Crew consisted of about eighteen, if I remember correctly. The skipper, sorry, commanding officer RNR was a lieutenant commander, our first lieutenant (also known as Jimmy the One, a slang term generally applied to that rank) was a sub lieutenant RNVR, and we also had a midshipman. The lower deck consisted of four engine room staff: two engineers and two stokers. The rest were two radio telegraph operators (sparks) one signalman (bunting tosser), one gunner, one radar operator and two wiremen: me and a Scottish lad called Coutts. The rest were seamen, ordinary and able. One became an able seaman after a year, subject to satisfactory progress.

I was now in 'Combined Operations' for which we were paid an extra half a crown per day 'hard lines money' because of the rather primitive conditions under which we lived. We also had to wear a badge on the left forearms of our uniforms, which consisted of an anchor, a 'tommy gun' and the RAF wings. I perhaps should add that we had to wear red embroidered badges on our everyday uniforms and I already had a torpedo on my left upper arm and, later, was to wear a killick to denote leading hand and one stripe to denote three years' service. A second stripe would have indicated twelve years but I couldn't see that. On our best uniforms, or 'tiddly suits' we could wear badges embroidered with gold thread. To us 'could' meant that it was practically compulsory, and I certainly do remember that these were very expensive, especially the Combined Ops badge.

There was no hot water, except when we heated up a bucketful on the coal-burning galley stove - needed for washing clothes (dhobiing) and a bath, consisting of two buckets of warm water with a foot in each bucket. Primitive, but effective. We could have had a shower after pumping up enough seawater. This, however, would have been cold and, whilst in harbour, was mainly dirty and oily so there were not many takers. What had been the crew's quarters when it was a Tank Landing Craft was split up into a wardroom for the officers and the rest was for the petty officers and the boatswain. The so-called lower deck crew's mess deck was a portion of what had been the tank space, the rest of this was fitted up with bays for the rockets. These were of three types: smoke, incendiary and high explosive, stored in that order starting from the stern. Of this, more later, as this fact saved all our lives. We slept, of course, in hammocks, which had to be lashed up each morning as soon as we got up and then stacked in a bay. There was not enough room in our mess deck to accommodate all the slung hammocks, so two or three of us had to sleep in the rocket magazine.

I suppose that conditions were not very hygienic, but everyone was scrupulous over personal hygiene and everything was scrubbed out daily. We also seemed to spend half of our lives washing and ironing. Now and then the quartermaster was given the order to pipe 'hands to make and mend' to enable us to take part of the afternoon doing our laundry.

I soon found out that one was expected to be 'Jack of all trades' on such ships and jobs, such as firing the Orlikan guns on gunnery practice, involved one also having to act as loader, chasing round the gun housing with a ready-loaded gun magazine. Doing quartermaster duty involved being in charge of the upper deck, slacking off or tightening mooring lines when necessary, piping the various calls of the day and ringing the ship's bell to keep track of the hour. The worst position one could get into was if the signalman was 'watch ashore' in the evening and you were signalled either by semaphore (using flags) or by Aldis signalling lamp, and you had to receive and reply to the message. Although we all knew both semaphore and morse code, we were by no means expert and the job took ages with constant calls for 'repeat' by those trying to communicate with us. In view of the fact that Royal Naval signalmen had the enviable reputation of being the finest in the world, it was embarrassing to say the least, especially as you could well imagine what they were saying at the other end.

I became appointed to the 'forrard party' when coming alongside or tying up to a buoy and I landed up with the jobs of heaving line thrower and buoy jumper. This involved having a coil of thin rope with a 'monkey's fist' at one end, weighted by being dipped several times in red lead paint and, in my case, with a steel nut inside that. Heaving lines were very personal things and I made mine of woven sennet line, which didn't kink and was only supposed to be used for the ships' log. In use, it had to be thrown ashore (or, at least, one end of it did), to be taken up by anyone who was about. The other end was tied, by using a bowline, very quickly to a bight (a loop) on the end of the mooring line, which was made of three-inch manila and was too heavy to be thrown. When this was secured to a bollard on shore, the rest of the forward party had to haul the ship into shore, while the same procedure was taking part at the stern. Tying up to a buoy was different in that the helmsman brought the ship in alongside it, then some idiot (me) jumped down onto the buoy and secured a line onto the buoy. When all was secured one scrambled back up the line and onto the ship.

I shall always remember the day before D-Day. We were tied up to a buoy in Southampton Waters and the skipper decided that, due to rough weather, we would double up on the bowline. I slid down the line onto the buoy, which was about four foot in diameter with a ring at the top. The idea was that one stood astride the ring holding onto the ring taking a second line and fastening on. There was not a lot of room there and it involved a bit of acrobatics. It was definitely a job best done by one person who knew exactly what they were doing. Despite this, the first lieutenant decided he would come down and help me. The task was eventually accomplished, in spite of his help. I could hardly have told him to get lost. The final insult was when he asked how we got back onto the ship. I told him that we had to shin back up the line and proceeded to show him how. I was walking back along the deck when there was an almighty splash and I dashed back to find he had fallen into the 'drink'. I couldn't do much to help, except give him a hand when he neared the deck, where he proceeded to tell me off for walking off and leaving him. I was mad enough to tell him that I hadn't asked him to come down and help me and that if he had thought that he couldn't get back on board he shouldn't have tried. I was then threatened with being put on a charge for insubordination, and wisely kept my mouth shut. Fortunately, nothing came of it, but I've an idea he got his own back some time later when I had jumped down onto a buoy as the ship was being blown sideways on to it. This had resulted in the buoy being spun round in circles by the ship's forward motion before disappearing under the ship and coming out on the other side. My only action was to dive into the sea and swim away as fast as I could in case I was dragged into the ship's propellers. However, all went well, apart from me getting soaked. I never found out who was on the wheel at the time, but I had my suspicions. The only consolation I had was that, when the first incident had happened, I was only wearing scruffy overall trousers and a jumper, whilst he was wearing full uniform.

Generally, however, officers and crew got on well together. In such confined quarters it was a necessity and the occasional argument could always be settled in the open tank space, ending in shaking hands and then forgetting all about it. I think, at the time, we were all looking on life as a new adventure and never realised the fact that we were in a war and that we could get killed or injured. I also think that we had started to grow up fairly quickly, so much so that when I came home on leave it felt like I was only on a visit.

We came from all parts of England and Scotland, including one from Southampton where we were mostly based, and one from Bournemouth, just down the road. I always found the different regional dialects extremely interesting and, sometimes, fascinating. I was particularly intrigued by the Londoners and their cockney accents, especially with their 'parths' and 'barths' and 'darnces'. At first I thought they were just trying to be posh. Our coxswain was another Yorkshireman, from Bradford, so we had a natural affinity. Even he spoke differently to me and would talk about 'brewing a gradely cuppa tay', whereas in

Sheffield we would say 'mashing a good cup of tea'. Most of the crew were quite taken with the odd Sheffield expression which I sometimes came out with. For instance, nobody had ever heard of the word 'nesh' and had no idea what it meant. 'Stop mucking about', sent them into fits of laughter, as did 'side-ing the table' and ' washing the pots'.

One of the lads who, I believe, came from Croydon, was pleased when I could explain a question which had puzzled him for ages. Apparently he had been sent to Sheffield on a fortnight's course on coil winding at a company called M. Bernands, who were electrical manufacturers of large electric motors and generators. He had been staying with the family of one of the other employees and had been puzzled with the frequent use of the phrase 'coil oil', but had never had the courage to ask what they meant. He was mortified when I told him was this was 'coal hole' which would have lead down to the cellar. Such colloquialisms didn't seem all that common around the country, although one young lad who came from the West country did surprise us all on seeing a battleship for the first time. The bows of such ships came down vertically and his surprised reaction came out almost as one word, 'Look-um-go-straight-up-

and-down-dun-um'. After I'd been some time on board, my mother used to say that I came home with a worse accent than when I went in.

Local items of food were another point of interest and they seemed never to have heard of, let alone eaten, black pudding, brawn, and tripe and onions. One had to forgive them, though, as most of them were southerners. We had two Scottish lads who were always going on about things Scotch. For instance, they went on about the fact that none of us had ever heard of 'scotch pancakes' and one went so far as to ask his mother to send him some to show us what we had missed. A parcel arrived after a few days and we all tried them. They were all right, but nothing to write home about. Then one lad pointed out that, on the outside of the packaged pancakes, it showed the manufacturers were based in London. This, of course, we never let them forget.

We lived well, being on 'canteen messing', which meant that we were allowed two shillings and six per day, and bought all our own food from either the naval stores or the NAAFI. Rationing almost didn't exist. If you were lucky enough to find a good cook and a good buying manager, who knew something about the various cuts of meat, you could live like lords. We always had a large joint every day and what was left went into the soup for the next day.

On board ship, we were entitled to 'duty free' cigarettes. The allowance was eight hundred cigs a month which, if we wanted the most popular, Senior Service (what else?) or Players, cost us sixpence per packet or £1 per month. The present cost is around £200. Ships Woodbines, another popular choice, which were much bigger than the civvy version, only cost fourpence ha'penny for twenty.

Chapter Six

Understanding the Natives

I think it would be as well, at this point, to point out some of the idiosyncrasies of naval language, namely the vocabulary and pronunciation.

Royal Navy: Commonly referred to as The Andrew

Sailor: A matelot (matlow). All sailors are called Jack.

Soldier: Pongo

Marine: Bootneck

Air Force: Universally referred to as 'Brylcream boys'

Bows: The pointy bit of the ship, up forr'd.

Stern: The blunt bit at the back or 'aft'.

Pussers: Anything issued from naval stores e.g. the tobacco ration was known as 'pussers tickler'. No self respecting sailor would ever think of going ashore in anything but a tailor-made suit, referred to as his 'tiddly suit'.

Rum ration: Naval rum was 'bubbly'.

Sippers: A sip of everyone's tot given to the sailor whose birthday it was. This generally meant that he had the rest of the day off, being in no position to work.

Splicing the Mainbrace:

A double tot of rum given to celebrate the King's birthday or other auspicious occasions.

Mess deck: Where the lower deck crew lived.

Wardroom: Where the officers lived. The skipper had his own cabin, a bit bigger than a shoe box, but not much.

The heads: The area where the toilets and wash basins were situated.

Killick: Admiralty pattern anchor but with straight bar across in the same plane as the flukes. This denoted a leading hand and Leading Seamen were known as killicks.

Galley: Kitchen

Deck: Floor

Deckhead: Ceiling

Companionway:

A passageway or corridor

Blue jean: Sailor's collar, so called after the material 'Bleu jaune', the French material denim, a corruption of the

French 'de Nimes', made in Nimes, nothing to do with the modern use which has come to mean the trousers made of this material. The collar was navy blue when new with three white stripes round the outside, which had to be washed several times until it was a faded blue and then fit to be worn.

White front: The short-sleeved white cotton shirt worn under the jumper. This also had a blue stripe around the outside of the square neck. This was changed to a navy blue long sleeved hard woollen jumper in winter.

Black silk: This was a thin silk sort of scarf about four foot long by about ten inches wide, which was folded in two lengthwise and ironed, again folded in three until it was about two inches wide. It was ironed again, until it was almost permanently welded into one piece and never washed again - after all, it was black! It was worn round the neck under the collar, down the back of the open front and tucked in a loop across the bottom of this front and secured by the ribbons secured to this loop by a bow. The ribbons then hung down about a foot and were finished in a fishtail cut. The black silk was meant to commemorate the death of Nelson.

Bell bottoms:

These were our 'bell-bottomed' trousers, cut so as to enable them to be rolled up over the knees when scrubbing the decks. They were fly-fronted, which means that there were two flaps about five inches wide, which came round the waist and fastened in front with three buttons, one flap incorporated a pocket. The fly front was the flap coming up and was fastened at the top with four buttons. This went over the wide money belt which was standard issue. This type of fastening was the standard method many years ago.

The uniform all sounds a bit fiddly, but was actually very warm and comfortable. The whole thing was designed to be turned inside out when off. The bell bottoms were folded from the bottom in seven creases, supposed to denote the seven seas, and then rolled up. The jumper was similarly turned inside out, folded and then rolled up. It all took very little space in one's kit and preserved the creases. Incidentally, American sailors wore what can only be termed a 'music hall' version of this uniform, which we thought looked a bit ridiculous.

Time Time aboard was denoted by the ship's bell, incidentally the short cotton rope fastened to the clapper for ringing the bell was the only rope on the ship, all the rest were lines (the steel anchor cable was a hawser). The day was divided into various 'watches': midnight to 4am, 4am to 8am, 8am to midday, midday till 4pm, then two dog watches of two hours each, called first and second dog watch, followed by 8pm to midnight. This effectively divided the day into seven watches, so that if you were on 'watch on' and 'watch off', which is standard when at sea, you were on different times each day.

The first hour of the watch was indicated by two bells. The second was four bells, the third was six bells and the fourth was eight bells. Simple. Who needed a wristwatch, which would only get wet?

Time was rung by the quartermaster, a job which we, the seaman branch, all took in order, dressed in full uniform complete with white belt and gaiters. The quartermaster was in charge of the upper deck and gang-plank and duties included keeping the mooring lines in order, loosening or tightening up according to the tide. He had a bosun's pipe around his neck on a white lanyard and had to pipe the daily calls such as 'hands on deck', 'hands fall in', 'lights out', 'rum up' (which was the most important of all) and, very occasionally, 'splice the mainbrace', 'hands to dance and skylark' (True. Honest!) and 'hands to make and mend' which was an extra chance to do one's washing or 'dhobiing'. The other I'll leave to your conjecture.

Chapter Seven
The American Enemy

Most of our time was now centred on rocket practice, which took place at Studland Bay, and we must have fired thousands of rockets into that pretty little place. I still don't much fancy making sand castles on that beach as I am sure there must be a number of rounds still buried there. We were ashore every other night, which meant a round of the pubs, and we all had our favourite ones. Southampton was full of forces personnel, both British and foreign. I must admit there was a general feeling of animosity towards Americans, and it was generally accepted that they were 'oversexed, overpaid and over here', which I suppose was a highly biased and unfair generalisation, as we found them to be sometimes 'not bad' individually, but collectively intolerable, bragging and full of 'bull' and, by and large, just not 'British'. They had their few pubs, which we kept away from, and we had the rest, which they entered at their peril. There was a peculiar situation at one pub, which was our favourite, in that there was regularly one American officer whose pub it was before we appeared on the scene and we became quite friendly with him, even to the extent of letting him buy the occasional round of drinks. This was done in such an unpatronising and untypical way that we could not, in any way, find offensive.

Most of the time we were fully loaded with rockets and must have had a considerable weight of high explosives on board, so we had to anchor out in Southampton Waters. There was a sort of bus service of boats which called regularly taking us ashore and bringing us back at regular times. These were naval cutters called trot boats, crewed by naval 'wrens', two in number, who were quite good at manoeuvring, although occasionally they would try and come alongside with the tide instead of against it, and then have to try again. This generally raised a small cheer from us passengers, but in good fun. One particular night, we were coming ashore, it was quite dusk with a bit of drizzle, when an American LCP (Landing Craft Personnel) loomed up out of the dusk and smashed into the side of our boat, which was made of wood, stoving in the side so much that we started shipping water. It then shot off without stopping. When we looked round the wrens seemed to have disappeared and we thought they had gone overboard, until they emerged from the rope locker in the stern, which was the worst place they could have chosen if we were going to sink. They were quite shaken, so two of the lads took over and brought the boat back to shore, with all of us sitting over the gunwale on the opposite side to the damage to prevent us shipping too much water. We arrived back safely but as you can imagine this, again, did not endear us to the Americans. What they did amounted to criminal irresponsibility, which would have resulted in a Court Marshal. To make matters worse we all had wet feet and trouser bottoms. It made one wonder whose side they were fighting on.

Chapter Eight
In the Drink

At weekends, when the weather was fine, we used to have the dinghy over the side, together with the carley floats and spend our time swimming in the sea. The only sounds were from the 'doodle bug' flying bombs occasionally buzzing overhead and we used to listen until the engine cut out and then for the big bang, wondering where it had landed. We often had dolphins or porpoises swimming round the ship, but we gave them wide berth. We didn't know much about such creatures then and they were a bit too big to argue with. What a way to run a war.

The beer down south was rubbish and was not improved by the fact that we, more often than not, had to drink it from a two-pound jam-jar due to the extreme shortage of pint pots. It was quite common to see small groups of sailors walking about with their own pint pots. The only tolerable drink was 'boilermakers', which was a mixture of half a pint of bitter, topped up with a bottle of brown ale. Mild was said to be all the drainings from the pumps and lager was unheard of. Men from the north knew their bitter whilst down south I don't think they would have known a good pint even if it had jumped up and bit them. Funny people.

At times the authorities didn't welcome our ship in their docks. I suppose that, if it had blown up, it would have made quite a mess. Funnily enough, we never gave a thought to this possibility, we were probably either too young, or too thick, to think of it. We used to be shunted off either to Poole in Dorset or to the Beaulieu River, which is near Lymington. This is a tidal river and at the end of the navigable part was a place called Bucklers Hard. I believe it was, or is, a favourite haunt for yachtsmen. A 'hard' is a hard landing, usually cement, which shelves gradually into the water and these were used for dragging a boat out of the water. Very many of these were built specifically for Tank Landing Craft. The ship could be eased onto the hard, the door dropped, and then be quickly loaded up with tanks and their crews in no time at all. We were often left out in the river, which wasn't very wide for a ship of our size. On one occasion, three of us decided to go for swim in the evening. Big Lofty was the first to get ready and swam off. He soon found out that there was quite a strong tide flowing, too strong for him to get back to the ship. He was about thirty feet away when he started to panic, and we shouted for him to swim for the bank instead of back to us. I don’t know whether he couldn't hear us or what, but he continued to drift away from us. I wasn’t being brave or foolhardy but, without thinking, I dived in and swam to him, which was easy as I was going with the tide. I managed to bring him to his senses, no doubt by calling him a stupid b******d, and we struggled to the bank. He was, by now, just about 'all in', what with his struggles. We walked along the bank to get topside of our boat, dived in and were back on board. Swimming finished. Would you believe, he never even thanked me, although I did remind him on one or two occasions that I ought to have left him, and that it was only because he was the cook that we couldn’t afford to.

Poole was another place where we weren't welcome, so they sent us out into Poole Bay, almost a small inland sea, which contained two or three islands, one of which was Brownsea Island, now the Boy Scouts' centre. These islands had been evacuated during the war and during the fine weather we rowed over to one of these where the orchards were full of fruit - apples, pears and plums - which made a welcome addition to our diet. Big Lofty must have got fed up with our constant demands for apple pie.

As I recall, Poole itself was only small with not many people about. The dock area was officially out of bounds to the Americans as they invariably finished up in the dock itself. We spent a Christmas there and, although a few went home on leave for Christmas or the New Year, most of us spent this time on board. We bought a thirty-six-gallon barrel of beer from a local brewery, after being invited to test a few of the brews before buying. This was duly set up in the wheelhouse, under lock and key, in charge of a pal of mine who came from Huddersfield. His parents kept a pub there and he knew all about spigots, bungs and spiles. The officers gave us a case of whisky and some bottles of gin for when we ran out. We were not keen on gin although it was the favourite drink in the wardroom. Of course, this was long before I discovered the delights of gin and tonic with ice and lemon - although I never lost the taste for rum. On New Year's Day we ran out of everything and, finding out that the officers were ashore, we invited ourselves into the wardroom where there seemed plenty of whisky left.

I don't remember much more, except that the next morning we were all on a charge. The first lieutenant said that they were not much concerned about us drinking the whisky, but objected to us pouring it out on top of the wireless set and treading broken glasses into the carpet (I don't think we did really), and as a punishment we were to have 'two and one' in future: the daily rum issue was to be dished out to the coxswain and then let down with two parts water. The issue was a sixth of a pint and, what with the added water, this made it half a pint. This, he knew, was a serious blow to us, and when the coxswain brought it below there were loads of glum faces, until he suggested we all have a good swig, top up again with water and he would then take it back saying that we refused to drink it. This he did and it had to be poured over the side in the first lieutenant's presence. Next day he relented somewhat and had it with equal parts of water, the same thing happened again and he couldn't stand any more. I think it hurt him almost as much as us. The following day we were back to 'neaters' and everyone was happy, although we were supposed to have the rum diluted, nobody had any idea why and, on small ships at least, this rule was not followed.

It was during the time when we were anchored in Southampton Waters, that I had an experience which taught me a big lesson – and it was nothing to do with alcohol. I was on quartermaster's duty between two and four in the morning. This and the next watch were about the most boring, and I thought that I would get the dinghy out - it was tied up to the handrail - and row ashore, about two or three hundred yards away, and go for a walk round. I did this and, after sticking the anchor into the mud, went on with my walk for about ten minutes. Just as boring, but at least it passed the time. On getting back to the dinghy you can imagine my utter panic to find that I had slipped up and the tide, still going out, had left the dinghy about twenty feet further up the bank. I was utterly scared as I knew that I would never get the boat back into the water. I imagined being there the rest of the night, then being court-marshalled and subsequently shot at dawn, at least, for desertion. However, I thought I had to try to move the boat and decided to, at least, make an effort. I worked like a madman and managed to move the boat a few inches, so, for the next two hours, furiously worked and moved it a few inches with each monumental push. Eventually, I was sweating like a pig and just about covered up to the waist in filthy mud. The hard work paid off though and I, at last, managed to get the boat into the water. I couldn't believe my luck and, after taking a few minutes to get my breath back and let my heart rate get to something like normal, I rowed back to the ship, tied up and just about collapsed onto the deck. I then had to strip off and get changed into clean clothes, hide my mud caked shoes, socks, trousers and underwear. I then woke the next one on watch, by which time it was seven o'clock. He queried the time, but I told him to shut up and that he was 'just lucky'. Never again!

Part Two

Fighting and Surviving

Chapter One
The Real Thing

OPERATION NEPTUNE

COMMANDING OFFICERS ARE TO CLEAR LOWER DECK AS SOON AS THE GATE IS PASSED AND READ THE FOLLOWING SUMMARY OF THE OPERATION TO THEIR CREWS.

Four years ago today, I was in the Bay of Seine in a light cruiser, endeavouring to evacuate the 51st Highland Division. Tomorrow we are going to land the 3rd Canadian Division in the same neighbourhood. The landing is one of five landings which are taking place along this coast. Force S are landing on our port side, and Force G is landing on our starboard side and two American forces are landing to the west of us. The whole assault is to be pressed home with the utmost vigour regardless of loss or difficulty.

There are a certain number of guns on Hitler's famous West Wall, but in our particular neighbourhood they do not amount to more than a dozen 6inch guns and about twice that number of 3inch guns.

There may also be some surface opposition during the night but as Force J has Force G on one side and Force S on the other side and a line of destroyers in front of us we probably won't hear more than a lot of bangs during the night.

The assault is the largest that has ever taken place, the following may give you some idea of its size.

4000 landing craft manned by 100,000 seamen will land 125,000 men and 25,000 tons of stores in Europe on Monday. On every succeeding day we are going to land 35,000 men and 25,000 tons of stores.

The initial assault, which is starting now, is supported by 6 battleships, two 15inch gun monitors, 22 cruisers, 70 destroyers, 180 craft of coastal forces, 200 minesweepers and 5000 aircraft. This is a far bigger force than we started the war with.

Tonight an Airborne Division of British troops is being landed to hold the main river crossings so that Panzer troops will not be able to interfere with the landings. The coastal belt is only being held by 2nd rate troops. The whole area will be bombed all through the night until 0520 in the morning, then the beaches will be bombed by medium bombers until 0615. Fortresses will then take over until 0645. They will drop 900 tons of bombs in the area which is being attacked by Force J. After that rocket fighters and fighter bombers will strafe the beach until troops touch down.

Concentrate on doing the job as you have done it so many times at Studland and you will wipe out the strong points which are our objective.

Good luck to you all. I hope there will be some beer when you get back to Southampton on Tuesday morning.

Signed,
J.Haigh.
Lieut.RN

Some time in May, it came through the 'bush telegraph' that the 'second front', as it was called then, was near at hand. Suddenly, Southampton Waters and as far as Portsmouth was chock-a-block with hundreds of boats like ours tied up to buoys, which seemed to have appeared from nowhere. Then, the ultimate. On the morning of the 5th June 1944, the skipper at the 'morning fall in' read out a statement outlining Operation Neptune to the assembled crew.

I cannot quite remember, after such a long time, what our reactions were at hearing what amounted to a bombshell. I think we just accepted things in a sort of matter of fact 'wait and see' manner. After all, nobody had ever been in such a situation before, but our training over the previous few months had set us in good stead.

Also, I believe that the navy is very different from the other forces. Each member is, in many ways, a technician. Even an ordinary seaman's job is to know all about navigation, communications, seamanship, knots and splices, and generally all that is involved in 'messing about in boats'. We were, generally, left to work on our own initiative. Each one of us knew what our duties and responsibilities were and just got on with them. There was more reliance on self-discipline than was the case in the army, where discipline was imposed on the soldiers. This made us somewhat of a special breed and, although we were all trained in drill and square bashing, this was only by the way, so that if any one of us had been told that he was going to undergo a twenty-five mile route march for no logical reason, he would have told the person ordering it to get lost, and damn the consequences. Also, none of us would have countenanced having orders bawled at us by a corporal or even a lance corporal from a distance of six inches or so, especially if it concerned a petty or ridiculous matter, such as whitewashing a heap of coal or whatever. Mutinies have happened in the past and the Lords of the Admiralty seem to have adopted a most sensible approach to the navy of 'if it works don't fix it'.

So, this was it. We had a war on. But the weather worsened, so 'D-Day' was put off for a day. The skipper decided that we should double up on the bowline. We were tied up to a pontoon, a sort of floating raft, and Lofty and I were delegated to take another line out in the dinghy. Getting out there was no trouble, as the tide took us straight out to the pontoon, and we soon finished the job. Rowing back, however, was a different matter, as it was a stiff pull, but we got back all right and I jumped back onboard holding on to the boat's painter. A sudden gust of wind then ripped the rope unexpectedly out of my hand and, within seconds, Lofty was thirty or forty feet away. He quickly got back onto the oars again and headed back, but unfortunately after half a dozen strokes, one of the oars broke in two - Lofty was a strong lad - and off he sailed into the horizon. Urgent radio signals were immediately sent off to our headquarters ship, as we didn't want to lose our cook and, about three hours later, Lofty was returned to us towed by a small army LCP, no worse for his journey and unworried by the experience. He said that, at one time, he had been out in the open sea without a ship in sight, but he had not been bothered as he knew something would turn up, a typical British Mr Micawber attitude.

This wasn't our only mishap as we set sail in convoy later that night. After about an hour or so, we developed a cracked cylinder head on one of the main engines. Well organised, we soon had a ship tied along both sides to tow us, and we were inundated with a horde of engineering officers and chief petty officers who replaced the cylinder head in double quick time, while we all kept well out of their way. Things got back to normal and we carried on regardless, wondering 'what next?' But we were invincible or, at least, we were green enough not to think otherwise.

We approached the Normandy coast as dawn started to appear and things seemed to be fairly quiet. All operations were governed by the radar. We had outline silhouettes of our target area and the ship had to be accurately positioned so that the radar picture lined up with the silhouette. The first rocket bank in the bows was comprised of only smoke and incendiary rockets which were fired in salvos of about ten. These were for sighting, for finding the right distance. Obviously, we had to be first into the beach as anything in the way of the forty-two rocket salvos would have been made short work of, so all the landing craft had to keep station on us. As we were coming in towards the beach I suddenly remembered that the safety wedges on the front banks had not been removed, thereby rendering them ineffective. I immediately told the skipper, as I was on watch on the bridge, and he told me to get up forward and remove them as quickly as possible, and not replace the flimsy safety caps. I vividly remember saying to the skipper, 'For God's sake don't switch on the master switch whilst I'm up there', and immediately dashed up forward and started the job, with my heart in my mouth and feeling terribly vulnerable. There were two safety switches, one on the bridge in charge of the skipper, and the other which my mate, or myself, looked after. Both these had to be switched on before any of the individual firing switches were operative.

I had done most of the bank when the skipper came over the loud hailer telling me to get back straight away. I got back in about two seconds flat with my heart beating fifteen to the dozen, scared and wondering what else could go wrong. I hadn't joined this lot to finish up being smeared over a length of a Normandy beach by our own people.

Within a few minutes, we started firing the rockets and it seemed as though all hell had let loose. You kept your head down. Deck sprinklers were on, keeping the whole deck awash with sea water, as the heat generated by the rockets was terrific. Even so, after the whole lot had been fired, the deck needed repainting with bitumen paint.

Each salvo of rockets was spread over the whole of the deck, as a high concentration might have split the deck open. As it was, after each firing, we had to replace dozens of electric light bulbs on the lower deck. As each was in a waterproof jacket, it was by no means a simple job. Furthermore, as the lower deck heads on the lower deck were covered with granulated cork and then painted, a lot of this was loosened and everything was covered by a light coating of white granules.

We, obviously, couldn't see our own rockets being fired, but we could see the other rocket ships in the flotilla on each side of us, spaced out over our stretch of the beach. The sight was truly awesome. As each salvo was fired, the whole deck was covered by a huge sheet of orange flame which stretched out behind the ship by at least two ships' lengths. There had been several fighter aircraft flying overhead and guns were being fired all over. A general signal was broadcast over the whole fleet's loud hailer, 'Cease firing. These are our own planes.'

A very sad event took place when one of our fighters flew into a salvo of rockets. There was a bright flash of an explosion and that was it. No wreckage seemed to be left to fall back to the sea. It had been the pilot's own fault as everyone had been strongly instructed to keep to the rear of the rocket ships but, nonetheless, a sad waste of life.

That was it. The rockets were all fired without any appreciable opposition, operation apparently successful. All that was left was to turn around and head back home, having cleared every obstacle from the beaches: barbed wire, mines, tank traps and effective opposition, or so we presumed, and we duly turned around and headed back through the incoming hoards of craft of all kinds: tank landing craft filled with tanks and soldiery, personnel craft full of wet and miserable-looking men who couldn't find any shelter from the sea spray - and the weather was still a bit rough. We also passed the much larger LSTs, with big double doors in front, a bit like our present-day cross channel ferries. Beyond all these were the bigger stuff: battleships, monitors, cruisers and destroyers, who could stand off at a distance and bang away.

However, before we reached these, we were instructed to anchor up and, after the enquiry of our esteemed superiors, 'Ey, ey, what's up then?' were told that we had been delegated to stay behind in case we were needed to go to the help of the Americans. Apparently, somebody somewhere had had his head screwed on the right way.

It turned out, eventually, that we were not needed. The Americans had become bogged down on their beach and were unable, or unwilling, to move inland on what was said to be the easiest beach of the lot, although this was later altered to read the most difficult, presumably to save face. This was a long time before they had made such films as 'Saving Private Ryan', which showed on film that the

Americans were extremely brave and effective, miraculously even in areas where they had never been! But, there again, what do I know? A lot of our history has had to be rewritten later, either for fact or for expediency, who can say?

Nothing much happened for the rest of that day. There were a few shells and flak flying about, making big splashes in the sea, but after a while, one could forget those. The only one to worry about, was the one that hit you, and we didn't get one of those.

That night, however, (I can't remember the time, except that it was dark) a massive American LST came looming up frighteningly close. It didn't exactly hit us, but stopped with its bows only feet away from our stern and then dropped its anchor. It was like precision bombing. Their massive anchor scored a direct hit on our dinghy, which was lashed across the stern, smashing it to matchwood and then knocking it over the stern where our anchor was. By this time, our skipper was up on the bridge on the loud hailer and what he didn't call their skipper isn't worth mentioning. His words were lurid and magnificent and almost lit up the night sky. It must have been heard by most of the fleet. I do remember that he said that he wasn't fit to drive a ******* pram. There was no reaction from them whatsoever. That is until the skipper bellowed out that we had two hundred tons of high explosive on board. Then things happened. They pulled up their anchor at top speed and it came up like a cork from a bottle. Unfortunately, it took up our anchor with it, snapping the anchor cable like a piece of string. The LST quickly retreated backwards at full speed, without us hearing a word from them during the entire event. I can only conclude that it was a ghost ship, really, and didn't have any crew aboard. Americans do seem to suffer from some unfortunate incidents.

In retrospect, I suppose that these could be said to be early examples of what has now come to be known as 'friendly fire' – or is it, perhaps, 'collateral damage?'

However there we were, deeply in the mire without an anchor and we had to start main engines so that we could hold station. The next step was to sort out the mess, clear away and ditch overboard the smashed up dinghy and see to the broken anchor cable with its badly frayed end, which involved cutting the cable back to a good state and splicing a new eye on the end. As anyone who has done the job will tell you, it's about the worst job in the world, involving hammer, marlin spikes and much cursing as one's hands are ripped to pieces by the black greasy ends of the cable strands, resulting in them, too, needing repair afterwards with much Elastoplast. Fortunately, I was not one of the two detailed off by the coxswain to do this job. I had done plenty of splicing using rope, but had barely touched cable. The ship had two Admiralty pattern anchors, one already at the stern but the other was right up in the bows, each too light to hold bottom, but we reckoned that the two fastened together might do this. We set about fetching the bow anchor, which had to be manhandled the full length of the rocket deck, skirting the rocket banks, and somehow scrambling it over the blast screen. It needed about six of us, but we managed it in about two hours or more. It was a miracle nobody was maimed although one lad had a badly gashed leg and I got two squashed fingers, which bled like a pig, the damned thing weighed at least half a ton or more. I wouldn't attempt to relate how we finished the job but it was a triumph of a combination of brute force, much inventiveness and jury-rigging, and we managed it, which was no small success. We eventually finished, dog-tired, filthy dirty, hungry and dead chuffed.

The skipper, bless his little cotton socks, gave orders to splice the main brace and we finished up with the tot of rum, bacon sandwiches and a steaming hot mug of tea. We quickly got washed up and scrambled into our hammocks and died. It had taken about three hours and we thought that the war would have to wait for tomorrow.

Tomorrow arrived with a bang, as we found that we had anchored about a quarter mile inland of one of the big monitors that started banging away at establishments on the mainland, whilst the mainland guns began to reply. Most of the shells seemed to be landing between ourselves and the monitor. The screaming of the shells passing overhead was truly horrendous and there we were, playing 'pig in the middle', not an enviable position to be in. The skipper immediately sent a signal off to our headquarters ship for permission to move our position, which was duly given, and we scooted off to a place nearer the shore.

There were several sunken and abandoned ships around us and the occasional body floating past, face down in the water. The sea, we noticed, seemed to be teaming with a myriad jellyfish, and I think that it then came home to us that this was what war was all about. Late morning, the signal came through that we were to take on another load of rockets, to be loaded straight into the rocket banks, keeping those already below in reserve for when we went to the aid of our American cousins. This took up most of the day and, as these rockets already had the fuses fitted, they had to be handled with care. Normally the fuse was screwed into the rocket nose just prior to loading. Our skipper, whatever his good points were, was not very good at coming alongside jetties and, consequently, we never seemed to have full set of guard-rails round the deck. There was usually some damage somewhere and it was whilst we were transferring rockets from the munitions ship tied alongside us, that I had a mishap. I was walking along the deck with a rocket cradled in my arms when the ship rolled, it was still a bit choppy, and I lost my balance and leaned against the guard rail which gave way and I fell between the two ships onto the catwalk which ran along the full length of the deck and about three feet below. As the rocket was fused, I daren't let go to try and break my fall. As I landed onto the catwalk with my right hand flat on the deck, unfortunately one of the fins at the base of the rocket chopped across the back of my fingers cutting them quite deeply. I sorted myself out and bandaged my fingers together. Penicillin had not got around to us yet and I used sulphanilamide powder, pressing it into the cut. After a shot of morphine, I had to carry on - but it hurt like hell and continued to do so for the next week or so. Later, it turned out later that I had broken a finger.

Loading was completed in the record time of about three hours and we then called it a day. The next day, we two electricians had to test the firing circuits for continuity, using an ohmmeter. If we got a bad reading, it meant scrubbing the brass contact plate at the rocket base and the spring-loaded trigger at the base of the rocket banks with a wire brush. A four and a half volt battery powered the ohmmeters and, as the rockets needed twenty-four volts to fire them, it was quite safe. Rumour had it that, on one ship somewhere, the battery went flat and they tried a 'megger' with a handle to crank at the side and produced two hundred and fifty volts which fired the rocket, and their electrician was duly fried.

The next day was reasonably quiet, but there was one amusing incident when we saw one of the massive parachute landings. Literally hundreds of big transport planes flew overhead in formation and we could make out, in the far distance, the parachutists being disgorged and the planes turning around and coming back. The planes were now back above us, when a solitary parachute was dropped over the sea. We all watched, open mouthed, and there was a spontaneous cheer from the whole of the fleet showing that a sense of humour could still exist at such a time. We would dearly have loved to have known the story behind it all.

Food was our next consideration, as we'd only expected to be over there a couple of days, instead of which, it turned out to be nearly a fortnight and we soon ran out of such things as bread, eggs and other perishable food. Lofty had thoughtfully brought some dried yeast, which I had known as 'barm' and, at home, was always in its live form. He tried to use it to make some bread which, all prepared, was put in a large meat tin and then into the oven. We finished up with, what can only be called, unleavened bread - about two inches thick and as solid as a rock, the reason for which proved to be that he had poured boiling water on the yeast, effectively killing it.

Naturally, we made Lofty's life totally miserable, pointing out that everybody knew that you had to use tepid water, not boiling, and asking hadn't he ever watched his mother making bread. Lofty took it all in good part, and we had to fall back on ships biscuits and dried egg, which was a very poor substitute. However, there we were, all alive, living a hectic life, not thinking of anything beyond tomorrow. After all, this was what we had all volunteered for. We were invincible, as happy as 'pigs in muck' and young enough and thick enough to believe it, praying that God grant us that nothing would happen to alter it.

Routine then set in. We managed to find a new dinghy from one of the disabled and badly damaged craft near us, which we retrieved by paddling over on a carley float. It proved to be a much superior to our old one, as it was a proper clinker built boat, whereas ours had been a typical wartime utility one, rumoured to be made of old tea chests. The weather, by now, was much better and we rowed over to a cruiser which was not too far away from us, to see if we could beg or buy some bread and other provisions. We were in luck and came back loaded to the gunwales with bread and other goodies, even sweets and chocolate. They were very interested in us, having seen us fire our rockets. I think that for some reason they felt sorry for us and told us to come back again when we ran out, if we were still about!

It felt funny when we had to change into proper uniform to visit a cruiser, instead of our usual motley collection of individual rigs. Such is fashion that our ultimate ambition was to obtain a French matelot's striped jersey, but nobody managed it. We did manage one or two trips ashore, though, which was very interesting. The war seemed to be going our way, so far as we could tell, but we were told not to wander about too much as everywhere was mined. Two of the lads came back with some cheese, but there were no vegetables to be had, as the local people were a lot worse off than we were.

The cheese looked like nothing we thought it should look like. It was in flat rounds, like a sponge cake, but covered by a layer of mould. When the mould was cut off, the cheese underneath didn't taste too bad, but it still looked a bit dodgy. The next day, however, it had started to run and smelt like sweaty socks. We decided it had 'gone off' and threw the whole lot overboard. It was many years later that we found out, as any youngster nowadays could have told us, that it was Brie. Clearly, some poor farmer from near Arromanche had given us some of his prize cheeses, which had been carefully hidden away from the Germans. On looking back, we felt guilty for the poor devils as at least we had never gone hungry.

Around that time, another thing we discovered, floating about in the sea, were literally hundreds of metallic sachets of what turned out to be Nescafe, something we had never seen before. The Americans had ditched them overboard, but we found them very welcome.

For the next few days nothing much happened. We seemed to be getting on well with the invasion and things, so far as we could find out, were going our way. Eventually, we were given to understand that we were not going to be needed by the Americans and were ordered to return back to Southampton, which we duly did. There, we found ourselves in the middle of much rushing about as numbers of troops, especially Americans, were being loaded onto landing craft for the journey over to France. The Americans, in particular, looked a motley collection, slouching along in their battle fatigues and apparently, to our surprise, wearing rubber-soled boots, the odd one or two dropping out to retie a bootlace or whatever, and a few seemed to carrying a guitar or piano accordion. Battle or picnic?

There were odd blocks of German prisoners of war standing about with a couple of British soldiers stood a few paces away, smoking and seemingly awaiting transport. The Germans appeared to be very downhearted and despondent, which was quite understandable, probably wondering what sort of treatment awaited them, and we were thinking that this would be probably much better than they thought. We witnessed a rather unsavoury incident when a small group of about half a dozen Americans were passing by. One of them started dancing about in front of the prisoners, laughing and mocking them, an attitude we thought was a bit beyond the pale and simply not done. However, things altered rather dramatically when a British army sergeant quietly walked up to the back of the American and, rather forcefully, kicked him up the backside. This abruptly ended his antics and, to our eternal shame, our crew raised a small polite cheer and the Americans went off rather shamefaced. I think that we all could have forgiven the Germans if this had evoked a half smile, but no. They maintained a typically stoic Teutonic expressionless mien. It takes all sorts!

The next few days were taken up with thoroughly cleaning ship, refuelling with diesel oil and coal and getting in further supplies of food for current use and replenishing our stocks - not forgetting the yeast - whilst the dockyard got on with replacing our big anchor which, what with cranes etcetera, was made to look a fairly simple job. We got on with the job of our washing and ironing, like the busy little housewives we were, and sampling, as per instructions, the Southampton beer. All the pubs in Southampton were full to overflowing, often with people standing outside.

My hand was still painful, so I was sent along to the sick bay in the docks, where I was given a note to take to the hospital in Southampton for an X-ray. This I did and it turned out that the index finger had been broken and was beginning to mend on its own. They fixed me up with what they called a collodion splint. This consisted of a thin layer of bandage painted over with a clear liquid which set hard in seconds. This process was repeated three times and it finished up as effective as a normal plaster cast, and that was that. I was walking away when the doctor told me not to get it wet, as the stuff was water-soluble. I thought to myself, I'm in the navy, at sea and having to do my own washing and I'm told not to get my hand wet. Aren't we alright! However, they say that necessity is the mother of invention and I soon found that those little things euphemistically called prophylactics, made by a firm called Durex, made an effective and waterproof covering. I only needed to change to a nice clean layer of bandage for shore leave.

Chapter Two
The Walcheren Landing

After messing about like this for what seemed ages, we finally received orders to sail to Ostende for another landing. As I recall, we sailed on what was a miserable day so we didn't pay much attention to what was happening 'up top'. We eventually arrived at our destination in the rain and found ourselves in a passageway between two massive woodcn jetties, presumably leading to the inner docks. We tied up to one of the jetties just under a large wooden signboard with the words 'Anchoren Verboten', which had been painted with fluorescent paint. This signboard eventually finished up adorning our bridge. I think it was a notice that perhaps might have been of particular use to us, had any American boats happened to come into our vicinity, but it was not needed as this was an all-British operation.

We spent several days in Ostende and spent most of the time investigating the very elaborate defences set up by the Germans. There seemed to be miles of underground passages fitted, about every twenty five yards, with a handle which, when pulled, set off a cluster of hand-grenades on the surface above. We also found an extremely sophisticated underground mortar thrower, equipped with a periscope, with which one could lob mortar bombs anywhere one wanted. Somebody eventually got this thing working and, as a result, mortar bombs were being lobbed about in all directions.

The first night, the lads went to explore and find out what Ostende was all about. They came back very disappointed as it appeared that the very popular(?) General Montgomery had decreed that all alcohol, with the exception of beer, should not be allowed to be sold and, incidentally, that the 'houses of ill Repute' were all to be closed. I think that the idiot thought that we innocent British were too unsophisticated to withstand such temptations and would be easily corrupted. I remember one lad, who was an inveterate boozer, saying, 'I've drunk sixteen pints of this Belgian, so called beer, and I'm still as sober as a judge.'

The boats which used to take us ashore and bring us back were manned by old Flemish sailors who only seemed to speak, I think it was called, 'Walloon' which seemed to bear very little resemblance to French so, as you could imagine, any attempt at communication was impossible and we got back to our own ship more by good luck than any other way. Whilst there, some of us borrowed a jeep, of which there were plenty around and, after we had managed to fathom out how the multitude of gears worked, we bobbied off to Bruges to have a look at their Manikin Pee fountain. It was quite an enjoyable afternoon out. When we got back to Ostende, we returned the jeep to where we had found it, and found that nobody had missed us. I think it was about this time that the first lieutenant came down onto the mess-deck one evening to tell us that our Lords of the Admiralty, in their infinite judgement, had decided that we, the crew, had been awarded some decorations for our performance and bravery in the face of the enemy. Instead of allotting one for each man, which would have been the obvious and fair thing to do, the allocation had been set at one 'Mentioned in Despatches' and one 'Distinguished Service Medal', and that these were to be awarded at the discretion of the officers. He pointed out that most ships crews had been told to settle the matter with a pack of cards. For instance, the men who drew the first two aces got the medals. However, our officers had decided that the two most senior members of the crew were to be considered as the bravest and as a result the chief motor mechanic and the radar operator were to get the medals, and that was that. The general opinion seemed to be that it would have been better not to have awarded any decorations at all, as it seemed that this scheme was debasing the whole idea.

This landing, designated as 'Operation Infatuate', centred on Walcheren, a very heavily fortified island, which was guarding the sea passage to Antwerp - and it was imperative that the Allies had sea passage to Antwerp to enable further penetration into Europe. This was to be a purely naval operation with the navy, naval commandos, marines and marine commandos, together with various other specialised services, which were not generally known about. The whole operation was to be helped by the R.A.F bombers who were to bomb the island heavily throughout the previous night. It sounded as though it was going to be a bit rough, and we didn't get any sort of pep talk this time. As far as I can remember, we set sail around dusk. In the event, however, the bombing did not take place, as it had been called off by the R.A.F due to severe adverse weather conditions. This decision turned out to be calamitous for the whole landing. In our opinion, we had been let down by the

R.A.F. I think that it only dawned on us then, that the reason that the Normandy landing had been, in effect, a piece of cake was that our type of craft, the rocket ship, had been a secret weapon. Now, the Germans, who were not fools, knew what we were, they were going to be suitably prepared in future. It proved to be so. They set up a tremendous barrage with their guns and, as the R.A.F. had not done their early softening up of their defences during the night, we were there like sitting ducks because we had to approach our objective at a slow speed and a fixed straight course governed by our radar. I think it was at that point that we really realised that war could be a nasty business and that we were going to very lucky to get away with it in one piece. Shells were landing all around us and only missing us by feet. They set up huge fountains of water, completely drenching both the ship and any of the crew who was out in the open. I do remember thinking, rather incongruously, though aptly, that it was a bit like the Charge of the Light Brigade, 'cannons to the left of us, cannons to the right of us, et cetera', and mentally calculating how many strides I would need to take before making a quick dive over the side. I decided to find a more sheltered place and made my way over to the quarterdeck and into the space between the galley, the skipper's cabin and the wheelhouse where most of the crew were - that is those who were not specifically on duty.

In a minute, the order came from the bridge to fire the rockets and this started immediately. The whole sequence was only to take a few minutes, and then we could about turn and get the hell out of it. Unfortunately, things didn’t turn out quite like that. We had just turned through a hundred and eighty degrees when we got hit. The shell, most of which we found afterwards, was a seven-inch amour-piercing shell – a type which didn't contain a lot of high explosive. It hit us dead in the stern smashing up the whole of the steering, then went through a steel bulkhead and across the after mess-deck. It then went through another steel bulkhead, which was re-enforced with a one-inch armour plate, and into the engine room where it created havoc by completely wrecking one of the two main switchboards, smashing the massive cast iron exhausts systems for both engines and one of the generators. This effectively disabled the whole of the electrical systems including lights and pumps, which were essential for the engine cooling systems, and the pumps powering the deck sprays, which counteracted the tremendous heat generated by the rockets. It then penetrated another armour plate, then continued its journey through the diesel fuel tanks, releasing hundreds of gallons of diesel, through the crew lower mess-deck, through the officers wardroom - creating even more havoc - completely smashing the ship's safe, starting one or two small fires *and* ripping the door off the rum locker, smashing one or two gallon rum jars and even setting alight their wicker surrounds. Not finishing there, it went through another steel bulkhead and completely obliterated the food lockers containing all the tinned food, tea, coffee and other dry food stocks. It continued its journey into the magazine racks of rockets, setting off three of them and setting fire to some tarpaulins stacked on top. As I mentioned earlier, due to the way the rockets were loaded, these were smoke rockets, the least dangerous, which is the reason I am still here today.

Getting back a little, as the shell went through the after mess-deck and through the armour plate into the engine room, we were all crowded together in a hatchway up into the space next to the galley. The first we knew, there was an enormous bang as it penetrated the armour plate and the galley space was filled with smoke and flames and pieces of shrapnel rattled round. The radar operator, who was standing just in front of me was hit by one, which completely smashed his knee. And Lofty copped for one in the middle of his chest, making a terrible mess there. There was a mad scramble out onto the quarterdeck and much diving for shelter as the shells were still being thrown at us. I went round to the front of the wheelhouse and sheltered by some lockers. I think that we were all, to some extent, shell-shocked as there were several instances of irrational behaviour. For instance, I was soon joined by one of the lads who wanted to know if I was alright and wouldn't accept my answer, 'yes', insisting on feeling me all over, until I told him to 'bugger off'. Next was the midshipman who seemed to have gone all to pieces, and I'm afraid I hadn't much time for him. Then came Lofty who also wanted to know if I was OK. I said I was, and asked if he was alright. By way of an answer he pulled his jumper down and said, 'Look at that.' There was a gory hole in the middle of his chest, with bone exposed, which looked a right mess. I remember I said, 'For God's sake Lofty, cover it up and we'll do something about it.' He was undoubtedly in shock, and we went back onto the quarterdeck to get him fixed up with a dressing and a shot of morphine.

I seem to recall that the first lieutenant then appeared with the news that there seemed to be a fire in the crew's mess-deck, so some of us went forward where there was smoke pouring out of the hatchway. He suggested (ordered?) that someone go down to see what the trouble was, so one lad went down the ladder and immediately shot back up again like a cork out of a bottle with the news, 'The ship's bottom has fallen out.' We were not convinced so, like an idiot, I slid down the ladder. I was not being brave, I just didn't think and, after all, someone had to go. About three-quarters of the way down the brass handrail each side of the ladder disappeared into jagged ends and I gashed my right hand quite badly and virtually fell the rest of the way. As we suspected, the bottom had not fallen out the ship, but the deck was covered about fifteen inches deep with a mixture of saltwater and diesel oil which was being washed about with the movement of the ship. We had lost all engines and were virtually dead in the water. The ship was bobbing about, wallowing hopelessly.

There was a small amount of light from the emergency low voltage batteries and so a certain amount of detail could be made out through the dense smoke. The first thing I saw was that our own personal kit lockers, which covered the whole of one side of our mess-deck, had been ripped away from the bulkhead. Everything that we owned had been tipped out and, what with the diesel oil, had been completely ruined. The same applied to our hammocks. I managed to wade through into the magazine and saw that there was a fire burning in some tarpaulins on top of the smoke rockets, so I climbed up on top, dragged the burning material onto the deck and extinguished the flames.

I sat down on top of the rockets and immediately got up, having burned by backside sitting on the hot metal. It was only then that I realised that I was not in a very safe position, although I suppose that nowhere on the ship was safer than anywhere else. Nevertheless, I got out of there pretty quickly, absolutely stinking of diesel. To this day the smell of diesel is enough to make my stomach heave.

I got back onto the upper deck and moved round to the quarterdeck to see what was what. Looking back, it seems that from then on things happened in a daze. In spite of all that was happening, a small detail struck me. As I emerged from below, there was a coiled up water hose on the raised part of the rocket deck which was behind the blast screen, and on this was what looked like a piece of liver. I remember wondering which careless person had meant to throw it overboard, missed and just left it there. It's funny how such little things like that strike one at the most inappropriate times. Back on the quarterdeck in front of me was the worst sight I has ever seen in my whole life. There was the coxswain on his knees in front of what remained of one of the crew, Frank Cairns. His face was the colour of dirty putty, while below his face was just an obscene mess. I found out afterwards that he had been making his way forrard from the quarterdeck and someone had suggested he go by way of the engine room. Frank was a regular time sailor and, in the proper navy, seamen and engine room staff kept to their separate parts of the ship, so he had never been in the engine room before. When he came to the hatch leading out of the other end of the engine room, he'd had difficulty opening the hatch as he was halfway up the ladder. It was then that the shell hit him in his middle. He had been virtually chopped in two.

I found out all this later, but for the time being I was faced with this horrible scene. The coxswain had been a butcher in civvy street, in the days when butchers did their own killing, and I suppose he was, to some extent, inured to such sights. He was trying to get the remains stitched up in his hammock and shouted to me to give him a hand. I just froze and stood there helpless. All that I could say was, 'I can't', whilst tears of shame filled my eyes. Nothing had prepared me remotely for anything like this particular task and I was not up to it. Looking back I think that cox realised the situation and, to save me further embarrassment, changed the order for me to take over one of the Oerlikon guns on the bridge and send down a man called Edwards who was somewhat older than me. I went up top and gave Eddie the message before strapping myself into the gun harness wishing to God that some German planes would fly over so that, at least, I would be able to do something.

I think, looking back, that we were all, in some respect, shell-shocked and were working on autopilot. Things were all a little hazy and the fact that each one of us had been given a generous tot of rum did not help. I found that now and then I couldn't help but keep looking down onto the quarterdeck and seeing what progressed. Frank had been stitched up in his hammock together with a couple of hefty shackles to ensure that he sank. He was then placed onto a stretcher and covered over with a new White Ensign flag, then all the crew were mustered to a burial at sea. The skipper read out the formal 'burial service at sea' to the accompaniment of a volley from six rifles. Frank's body was slid out from under the ensign to land with a splash into the sea, which was by this time quiet rough.

The telegrapher had been sending out SOSs for help and, before long, a ship came into view. Whether it was a destroyer, a corvette or whatever, I can't remember although, thinking about it, it must have been a destroyer as anything less would not have had its own medical officer. We realised that the sea was too rough for them to come close alongside, so they sent over the ship's boat rowed by six sailors and accompanied by the ship's medical officer.

Their boat came alongside with difficulty and, after a tremendous struggle, we got the radar operator, who'd been seriously wounded, on board, strapped into a body stretcher. He was, by now, unconscious, through both shock and morphine injections. Lofty, however, was a different matter and was not quite 'out'. When he saw their boat bobbing about crazily, he grabbed our guard-rail and nothing could make him let go, until their medical officer smashed his knuckles with a wooden marlin spike. His fingers slowly uncurled from the guard-rail and he was unceremoniously dumped into their boat which then sheared off and they struggled back to their ship, glad to be out of it. We didn't see Lofty again for a good few weeks.

From then on things were pretty hazy. I got busy in the engine room trying to make some order of the main switchboards and managed to switch over some of the essential circuits for things like lighting and pumps, and whatever else I could manage, onto the remaining undamaged switchboard. I then started up. To my utmost relief and everyone else's, apart from a few sparks, things worked and the rest of the crew raised a small cheer which, to some extent, made me feel that I was not completely useless.

Things would have been pretty dodgy drifting about in the night with no navigation lights, but that was only a part of our plight. Fortunately we were drifting away from land and the constant barrage of guns, but beyond that we realised we were, as it is said, 'up the creek without a paddle'. We occupied our time ditching overboard all our personal kit, clothing and hammocks, whilst the chief motor mechanic managed to get one or two pumps working and the level of water and fuel oil gradually lowered. Apart from the mess in the magazine deck, we found that several single wardrobes, which we had unofficially relieved the Germans of, had been overturned and our overcoats tipped out into the oily seawater. I was particularly annoyed at this because they included my beautiful wool gabardine raincoat, which I had bought at great expense only two or three weeks before from Cole Brothers. Ratings were allowed to wear gabardine coats, but they were not supplied so, if you wanted one, you had to buy it yourself. However, we soon forgot trying to salvage anything and it all went overboard. I wondered several times if all this stuff was eventually washed up ashore and, if so, what the finders made of it all.

The next thing was that another rocket ship came into view with the intention of attempting to tow us back to Ostende. Due to the rough seas, they daren't come alongside, as both ship and engines were not designed for this sort of job. We messed about for ages trying to get a line between the ships but without much success. They managed to float a grass line down-wind to us, but as soon as we tried to tow it in and get a proper line, one of the ships lurched and the line snapped like a piece of string. The whole idea had to be abandoned eventually and the other boat, after wishing us good luck (no doubt glad that they were not in the same situation), sailed off into the distance promising that they would chase up further help for us. Our skipper decided that we should take things easy, and call it a day. We were all tired out, wet through and stinking of diesel oil and, by now, pretty hungry. Lofty's emergency replacement came up trumps with piles of bread and jam and gallons of hot tea (albeit with Carnation milk) which went down like magic, doing at least something to restore our spirits. The next thing was sleep, for those for whom it was at all possible.

Things were pretty grim. There was nowhere near enough space under cover for us all, even packed up together head to toe, and the best I could manage was the top half of me in the galley and my bottom half out in the quarterdeck, with the edge of the watertight door frame of the galley stuck into my middle. This was about two inches high and was hardly what one would call comfortable, nevertheless, in spite of all this, I did manage to drop off to sleep, even if only for a short time. Morning came eventually and the best you could say about it was that it wasn't raining.

Breakfast was the same as usual, except that the tea was fortified by a shot of rum, and we decided that we would continue disposing of all the ruined stuff and see if we could find any tinned food we could rescue from the magazine. We found plenty of undamaged tins, but the labels had been washed off so we didn't know what we'd got until the tins were opened. I did know that we weren't going to be short of tinned peaches.

One great find was several cases of what turned out to be tinned tomatoes and tinned bacon - red lead and bacon - which was always welcome. I managed to get the coxswain on his own for a minute and started trying to apologise for letting him down the previous day. To my utter relief he let me down lightly, saying something like, 'Forget it Fred. I have. I should never have asked you. After all, you were the youngest lad aboard, and who was the silly bugger who was first to go below and put out the fire in the magazine? Forget it.' For me, the relief was immediate. I had been thinking of it all night, or at least most of it.

All that day was spent clearing up some of the mess, plugging some of the holes in the ship's side. Somebody said that they had counted eighty-six holes of various sizes. Nevertheless, the level of water down below had been reduced to two or three inches and, to cheer us up, the weather was slightly improved. The whole day was spent in this manner with still no signs of rescue and we were becoming a little despondent. It was, perhaps, just as well that the first lieutenant didn't tell us that we'd been floating about, for what turned out to be three days, in a minefield.

On the third day, after we had spent most of our time trying to clear away the rest of the mess, and wondering what was going to happen to our ship, and whether we should ever get back to some sort of proper normality, another craft appeared on the horizon. This turned out to be an ocean tug that had come to our rescue. As you can imagine, it was welcomed with heartfelt thanks and a rousing cheer. In no time, we were all tied up alongside with lines which seemed to be about a foot thick, and soon we were on our way home or, at least, to Ostende. After watching the operations for some time, interest waned and we retired below to catch up with having a good wash and getting something to eat.

Chapter Three
The aftermath

I can't remember how long it took for us to get to Ostende, not that we were particularly interested. We eventually arrived back to our previous berth where, at least, we were thankful that we were not bouncing about. It's surprising how much worse this is without engines. The officers went ashore to report and try to arrange some sort of clothing for the crew, some food and, most importantly, some money. It turned out that the bundles of Belgian francs which had been in the ship's safe had been destroyed by the fire, together with all its other contents.

In due course, the first lieutenant arrived back with money, a certain amount of basic foods and army battledress (complete with Royal Navy shoulder flashes which had to be stitched on before we could go ashore), and the news that within two or three days we would be going home by troop ship, with the exception of a skeleton crew of three who would be kept for when the ship could be towed back to Southampton. The grapevine said that although the landing had been successful, we had suffered fifty percent casualties so it was a dearly won victory. One of the other rocket ships had been sunk and another like us had been badly damaged. We also heard that one of the gunboats, with a crew said to be in the region of ninety (which was what they had been designed for) had sunk in the shallows. Before they had fired a single shot, they had been completely destroyed by the Germans who had turned on the beach flame-throwers. The crew, consisting of mainly Royal Marines, had been wiped out to a man. Yet another secret weapon that had turned out to be not very successful.

I couldn't vouch for the truth of these stories, but this was what we heard. We were also given to understand that rocket ships were not in favour as, apparently, one of them had, like us, been hit by a shell just as they were firing their rockets. The result was that, as the ship slewed round out of control, a salvo of rockets was fired and landed on our own boats. Whether this had caused any casualties, or not, we did not know.

The next day we were told that we were going home the following day and we were to muster our kit together. Mine consisted of a German hand grenade case, used for holding stick hand grenades, and was about the size of a small attaché case. This contained all my worldly goods: a pair of socks, a change of underwear, about 400 cigarettes and a bottle of Navy rum. I had also bought, only that day, a 28-pound case of grapes, which were virtually unknown back home.

The following day, with the exception of three of the crew, we embarked onto the troop ship, together with what seemed like a couple of hundred soldiers. The latest good(?) news was that the Germans had developed the 'magnetic mine' and that many of our boats were being sunk without any sort of warning. This latest news was not received at all well, and most of us quickly developed a sudden preference to remaining in Belgium until the matter had been sorted out. Needless to say, off we went home, or so we hoped.

We had all been dished out with hammocks but no mattresses, and so the entertainment of the evening started. Some of the army lads started to sling their hammocks from the hooks in the deckhead. It was only understandable that, not having been shown the way to proceed, there were some amusing instances of lads swinging into their hammocks and the next minute finding themselves on the deck, which they discovered was pretty hard. It finished up with us giving demonstrations to groups of pongos on the proper way to do it. Eventually, we were all settled down with a silent prayer that the Germans had run out of magnetic mines.

In spite of having no mattress in my hammock, I slept like a log and, in the morning, we all found out, with some relief, that we had not met with any magnetic mines in the night and that we were back in Southampton again, this time in the local naval base. They didn't seem to know quite what to do with us, so sent us on a fortnight's survivors' leave and the next minute we were walking out of the base with all our worldly goods. There were a few minutes of panic when we were stopped by the guard with the greeting, 'Where do you think you lot are going?' Our reply, to the effect that we were going on leave, didn't cut any ice and his next remark was, 'Not dressed like that you're not'. Panic set in. I knew that if I was found with a bottle of rum and all those cigarettes in my hand grenade case I was up for the high jump.

I left any further argument to the others and was very relieved that, after they had forcibly argued that we were survivors and the army battledress was the only kit we had, the guard relented being, by now, not quite sure about his grounds in these circumstances.

He told us to get out quick before he changed his mind so, before anyone could say, 'Jack Tar', we were halfway down to the railway station (which everyone nowadays seems to want to call a train station for some reason). I was on my way back to Sheffield.

I arrived home sometime in the early morning when everyone was fast asleep in bed. Try as I might, I couldn't wake anyone and finished up climbing up onto the front bay window as I could see that the little top window was partly opened. I climbed onto the roof of the little porch which gave me access to the window. All I had to do then was to wake my brother and for him to open the lower window and I was home and dry. This was easier said than done for, although I'd taken off my collar, then my jumper, and rolled them up into a parcel which I'd thrown in at him, I could do nothing to wake him up. I finished up by somehow managing to climb through the little window. In no time, I was in bed and fast asleep and nobody knew anything about it until next morning. If I'd been a burglar I could have cleared the whole house. It was fortunate that burglars were not so thick on the ground in those days.

I found out then that my mother was in Claremont Nursing Home and, as all the rest of the family was either off to school or off to work, there I was all on my own with nobody to welcome home the conquering hero.

After having to make my own breakfast, I set off to find Claremont Nursing Home, which was then somewhere near where the Hallamshire Hospital is today. Eventually, I found it - and my mother - who, in spite of the French landings, had not been worried. She had worked out that I was somewhere out in the Far East because, in my last letter, I had mentioned that I was feasting on grapes and peaches. Letters were, of course, censored and no mention could be made of any, perhaps sensitive, information.

I think that the Claremont was entirely staffed with nuns in those days and I was welcomed like the returning hero and invited to stop for tea: wafer thin sandwiches with the crusts cut off, a right healthy meal for an invalid. That day, because I had taken them with me, everyone also enjoyed the very welcome and surprising addition of grapes.

As well as tea, I was also given a silver medallion, which, on closer inspection, I could see was a St Christopher, with the strict instruction that I had to wear it around my neck at all times and it would ensure that I wouldn't be drowned. 'Ah, well,' I thought, maybe it was worth a try. Looking back it must have worked.

It was not much of a leave with none of my friends about. I even did some gardening. It was almost a relief when it was time to go back to my ship, which I found was still in a mess. Beyond replacing all our kit and getting a new suit made, there was nothing to do, especially with the ship constantly full of dockyard workers. We were sent on another ten days leave - and so it went on.

Eventually, we were allowed back aboard, although things were still pretty messy with dockyard 'maties' still working there and air hoses snaking all over. We were constantly being moved about to different berths. One time we were shifted to a tidal dock. We had just managed to get tied up by mid afternoon when I was handed a couple of wires. Upon enquiring what they were for, I was told that this was our power supply, needed for when the tide was out and we could not use our own generators.

It turned out that this was only 110 volts AC and not the 240 volts DC that we needed. Panic immediately set in as I set to, trying to mock up a connection board with links to the various circuits that were essential. It was getting dusk and here was

I juggling about with a handful of wires and trying to make sense of things. To my everlasting shame, and painful recollection, as I only had two hands (and needed three), I stuck one of the wires in my mouth. It happened to be a live one and it felt just as though the dentist had gripped my teeth with a pair of pliers and was shaking me bodily by my teeth. It wasn't the only electric shock I have ever had, but it is certainly the one I still remember. However, it was all grist to the mill and, beyond leaving me in a cold sweat, I was still alive. As the old saying goes, 'worse things happen at sea.'

Another rather nasty thing happened to me which, this time, was not my fault. The 'powers that be' had decided that the method of charging both the engine starter and the rocket batteries was not safe and, without going into technical details, the dockyard engineers had fitted electrical cut-outs into the charging circuits. This was a very good idea as there had been several nasty accidents when making the necessary connections for charging the batteries. The first time I tried to make the connections nothing happened, except a loud hum. I got my test lamp and leads to check the connections and started various procedures. It transpired that the dockyard had connected up the cut-out wrongly, resulting in the whole thing blowing up in my face. It singed both my eyebrows and hair, but, worst of all, my hands took the full force of the explosion and the whole of the back of my hands were burnt, shrivelled and also copper-plated from the melted wires.

I don't remember much after that. The next I knew I was waking up in Southampton General Hospital, in terrific pain. I was in there for about ten days before they would let me go. For the first couple of days in the hospital, as I couldn't use my hands, a nurse fed me and I felt like I was a babe in arms again. After that, the nurse bandaged a dessert spoon to my hand so that I could, at least, feed myself.

She then, very solicitously, enquired how I managed going for a wee, and said if I found it difficult I was to give her a shout ... At this point, I awaited the rest of her sentence expectantly, but she finished by adding, '... and I will get one of the other lads to help you.' The imagination can work overtime at times.

When I rejoined the ship I found that a new cut-out had been fitted and wired up properly, but nobody said sorry. I suppose common sailors are a bit expendable.

I can't remember the date but eventually, after hearing that the war was progressing in our favour, it was announced that The Axis, that is Germany and Italy, had surrendered and the following day was to be known as 'V.E. Day' (Victory in Europe) and was to be a public holiday.

Naturally, this was the only topic of conversation and the speculation as to what would happen now was the main interest. There was still Japan to contend with, but we didn't come to any great decisions as to what next. The following morning the order was given that the whole crew were to assemble on the quarterdeck where the skipper would speak to us. This we did and he explained that we had just received a signal telling us to proceed to sea and anchor up to a buoy in Southampton Water. He added that we might be pleased to hear that he was ignoring the order and, instead, we were to clean ship and then all assemble in the wardroom at eleven o'clock. Wondering what this was all about, we duly did as instructed and gathered outside the wardroom at the appointed hour. We were warmly invited in by the skipper who, to our complete surprise, was unusually quite affable. He gave a little pep talk, saying how we had all done brilliantly and how proud he was to be our commanding officer. I think that, to some extent, we were all rather embarrassed, but he soon shut up and announced that there was more than enough whisky and gin and he would take it as a compliment if we would forget all about rank and do our best to make a big hole in it. 'Rum up' was to be piped at mid-day and, after that, he had no doubt that we would all like to go ashore and join in the celebrations. This raised a small cheer and we got down to serious drinking. Mid-day came and 'rum up' was piped by the first lieutenant, who himself was hardly in a fit state so to do.

We all dispersed, some to get our heads down for an hour as we were all in various states of inebriation. The rest of us got dressed up and made our way ashore, carefully negotiating the narrow plank between the ship and the jetty. There were about half a dozen of us together and we dropped into the nearest pub and ordered pints all round. To our complete delight we were told that sailors' money was no good that day and, by courtesy of the landlord and the regulars, all drinks were free. We were all very touched by this gesture and mumbled a, no doubt, quite inadequate thanks and got stuck in. We soon realised that this arrangement was pretty general in the town, as the word got around, and it struck me that, although sailors must have been nothing but a damned nuisance at times, at least to some people, we were appreciated.

A few weeks later the skipper sent for me and told me that I was leaving the ship and being drafted to Middlesborough where a new rocket ship was being built, specifically designed for the job, and I was needed there in order to familiarise myself with all the new electrical systems being installed. I was to live in civilian billets and I would be on my own, but was expected to be fully conversant with everything for when the ship was commissioned.

So, I set off to Middlesborough, which was quite a journey and, to rub salt in the wounds, the train stopped at Sheffield for about twenty minutes. For all I knew, it might have been a couple of hours, and I could have nipped off home for a bit. Anyway, I didn't risk it, stayed on, and arrived at Middlesborough with all my baggage which I had to leave at the railway station. It was fortunate that I also met the Chief Petty Officer Motor Mechanic who had also been sent on the same mission as myself. We found out we had to report to an office which had been set up in the town, Middlesborough not having a naval base. We were directed to our billets, which had been taken over by the navy but were still labelled 'Railway Buildings'. All it was, was a huge office block with dozens and dozens of rooms, each set up with two or three two-tier bunks on which to lay out our hammocks and nothing else. The ground floor had been set up as a canteen and was staffed with civilian women cooks who, as I remember, were very good so we had first-rate meals.

Every morning, I used to go down to the ship after a leisurely breakfast to see what was going on. There was an awful amount of entirely new equipment – all the latest stuff. For a start we had pointed bows which made it look more like a proper ship. Then there was electrical steering, capstan, refrigeration, cookers, electronic firing for the rockets, and a central heating system which, incidentally, we never found out how to get working. I had my own separate workshop, which soon came to be known as 'the cigarette lighter factory'. There was loads of other stuff, of which the most daunting was a gyro-compass system with two repeaters in different parts of the ship: the bridge and the wheelhouse. The equipment was housed in a separate cabin and looked exceedingly complicated. The only people allowed access were to be myself and the flotilla electrical officer. The worst aspect however was that to start up the system took the whole of four hours with various sequences to be tackled at set times. It immediately struck me that this meant that if we were sailing at 8 o'clock in the morning, I had to be up at 4 o'clock to 'light the fire', so to speak. The magazine was the height of sophistication. There was an electrical conveyer system to take the rockets the whole length of the magazine, an electrical conveyor lift to then take the rockets to the upper deck, and a final conveyor to transport the rockets the length of the upper deck which could be stopped wherever. The entire set up was brilliant.

The flotilla electrical officer spent some time with me going over the starting procedure for the gyro-compass (while, incidentally, impressing on me the expensiveness of it all) otherwise I was left to my own devices. It was heaven, I was lord of all I surveyed, so to speak.

I was quietly impressed with what I saw of Middlesborough. On the first day of my arrival there, I and the chief, as he would normally be addressed, went for a walk round the town. I think that it was a Sunday. There was a public park in the middle of town and, walking along, I felt a tap on my shoulder. On turning round, I saw a couple of pretty young girls quietly giggling to themselves. I should explain that it was a very old custom, I don't know whether it still is, to touch a sailor's collar to bring good luck. We got into conversation with them and found out that they were both studying music at college. We found out something else, too, and couldn't quite believe our luck. It turned out that, due to the war and other things, women outnumbered men by about seven to one, and the business of touching a sailor's collar was a convenient method of getting acquainted. The girls were, apparently, on their way home, but we made a date with them for the following week, and went away even more pleased with our new temporary home. Unfortunately, there was not a happy ending to the romance as, two days later, we both were sent on a fortnight's leave and, as we had no means of getting in touch with the girls, we never saw them again. Hard lines but, as the old saying goes, there are plenty more fish in the sea.

I soon made the acquaintance of another young lady who worked as an usherette at the big cinema in town and this turned out to be very convenient, as I quickly became known to all the usherette staff and never needed to pay to get in. As a result I saw all the films at least twice a week. One could say that a lot of our courting was done in the back seats of the cinema, unknowingly at the expense of the management. Although I got to know her quite well, I'm damned if I can now remember her name.

We ended up spending some considerable time in Middlesborough and gradually the rest of the crew joined us, including three or four from my previous ship. The new ship, by the way, was designated LCSR 1, short for Landing Craft Support Rocket No.1, the first of its kind and, incidentally, the only one.

I should mention that I had one near miss around that time. We had just got a new skipper who, we surmised, had not had a command previously and meant to show everyone how a ship should be run. He started off with having all the crew exercise before breakfast, and we had to run up and down the rocket deck. What with the rocket banks, which took up most of the deck, there was not enough room for all of us to run and it degenerated into a shambling walk. I think that the dockworkers were a little amused, but we weren't. It didn't go down at all well. The next thing was church parade on Sunday. We didn't mind church, but being marched round the town was a bit more than we could stand. Having said that, we couldn't do much about it. I was so fed up, that I put in a request to the skipper for me to take up my original plan to be trained as an officer. He called me into the wardroom after a day or two. The first lieutenant was already there. He asked me if I was serious and, when I replied yes, questioned me as to why had I left it until now to start thinking of this move. This rather put me on the spot and I thought, 'in for a penny, in for a pound', and asked if I could speak frankly and in confidence. He seemed a bit nonplussed, but said yes and I set off. I said that, to be honest, I didn't want to go and that my main reason was that I thought that this was no longer a happy ship. I pointed out that I thought we could be considered a crew who were all friendly with each other and who, in our opinion, were professionals doing a good job which had been appreciated, but that now, what with morning exercises and church parades, we were being made to look foolish - although I was quick to add that I was sure this was not intended. I ended by saying that I was sure that I was not alone in such thinking.

I finished with some trepidation, wondering what his reaction might be, but all he replied was that he would think further on the matter before passing my request onwards. A day or two after this, the first lieutenant took me to one side and told me that he thought that I had stuck my neck out a bit too far. The skipper had asked for his opinion and he had replied that, apart from the fact that he thought I ought to be shot at dawn, there was a certain amount of truth in what I had said, and he certainly would agree that in all we were a very good crew, especially in view of what we had all been through together. He finished up by saying that this conversation with me had never taken place and somewhat subdued I walked away. I was left with the thought that I had not got anywhere and things did carry on the same for another week, then exercises and parades finished without anything further being said, and I never breathed a word to anyone else.

While at Middlesborough we used to draw our stores, that is foodstuffs, from North Shields. I went once and decided I would try and buy some fish so we made our way down to the fish dock. Fish were being auctioned on the quay but we couldn't get anybody to even talk to us. Then one old sailor said that, once the fish was landed, it was in the auction and if we wanted any fish, we had to get down onto the boat. I went down trying hard not to get covered with fish slime and fish scales. I spoke to one old chap and asked about getting some fish. He said that most of it had been landed but he came up with a whole sack of plaice, every one as big as a dinner plate, and all he would take was a couple of packets of cigarettes. We dined sumptuously but eventually one gets very tired even of plaice, although it was very nice while it lasted.

Among the few girls I got to know there, I remember one of them very well. She was called Emily, Little Emily, and she and her friend, who was seeing a mate of mine, both worked at a big shoe shop in town. I remember one particular occasion when my mate and I were invited to Emily's home for Sunday tea. (Feet under the table.) To my everlasting shame whilst all sitting around after tea - it must have been due to the heat in the room - I fell asleep with my head on her shoulder. I hope, even to this day, that the family put it down to my being overworked. Well, it wasn't very complimentary of me, was it?

Another thing not to be proud of was that, being in civvy billets, we had to contribute something towards the cost. Our pay, which wasn't a lot to start off with, became less and, although we were later re-imbursed, it didn't leave much for us to live the high life. It was not unknown, if we were going out for a drink at night, for the girlfriend to slip over a ten bob note to help with costs, which took some getting used to. Most weekends on Sunday, if the weather was fine, we went by train to the coast for a picnic on the sand dunes. It was only a couple of stations down the railway line.

We were becoming quite domesticated, which in itself was quite a worrying thought, when we heard that, when the ship was finished (we were, by now, undergoing sea trials), we were off out to the Far East for the war against Japan, making the journey in some sort of a floating dock. One night around then, when we'd got back to our digs after we had been out on the town, I had just started to undress when all hell let loose. All the church bells starting ringing and all the ships in harbour were sounding off at full blast. Puzzled as to what it was all about, we were soon made aware as quite a crowd had gathered outside the building shouting for us to come down and that the war was over. My first thoughts were that there would be no Japan. It had obviously been at the back of my mind as something we were definitely not looking forward to. My next thought was to get dressed again and get outside to join in the celebration.

Everyone made their way to the Civic Hall where an impromptu stage had already been set up and a band, which had been playing there all week, was in full spate. Everyone was dancing and were obviously more than delighted at the news. It seemed as though most of the crowd had just put a coat on top of what they were wearing - or in some cases weren't wearing - and just went out. One just got grabbed and dragged into the festivities. The intent of a lot of them was obviously on fraternisation - and who were we to gainsay? I think that a lot of fraternisation went on that night and I have often wondered if the population figures showed an unusual peak some nine months later. Nevertheless it is not very often that we have an armistice happen, so at least it was all in a good cause.

All things must come to an end and we eventually got our sailing orders. We were off to Inverness and then were to proceed through the Caledonian Canal, which cuts right through Scotland and comes out on the west coast. There were many protestations of undying devotion and promises to write regularly, which I suppose were meant at the time, although I don't quite agree with the old age adage that 'absence makes the heart grow fonder'.

It perhaps was a good thing that we were off, especially after Emily's father casually mentioned that if I decided to settle down in Middlesborough, now that the war was over, he could find me a good job as an electrician with the firm he was connected with. It struck me later that this was perhaps a 'fishing venture'.

About a week later we set off for Inverness in the early morning and, as the day developed, the weather worsened and became a storm. We found that there was at least one design fault in the new ship. The fact that we were still flat-bottomed made it impossible to keep to a course in rough weather and, when at the helm, it was constant attention and work as we were blown off-course by as much as twenty degrees. It was a bit like trying to steer a sledge on an ice rink. We arrived at Inverness in the evening after a rough journey and found out that the powers that be would not let us into the harbour. They considered that, due to the weather, which was blowing quite a gale, it was too dangerous. We had, therefore, to anchor-up at sea, which was not a particular welcome thought. It meant that a close watch had to be kept on the anchor cable and, as it was, twice during the night we had to weigh anchor and re-set it as we were dragging the bottom. In spite of all this, the weather had calmed by morning and we entered harbour. We took things easy for an hour or so and enjoyed a welcome, but late, breakfast before we made our way into the Caledonian Canal entrance. It turned out that we would be, if we made it, the biggest vessel to go through the canal and, according to details we had been given, we should have to position ourselves at a slant inside the many locks we would encounter. And so it proved.

It was a peculiar sensation to find ourselves sailing along with very little space on either side between us and the bank, and to see cows, sheep and green fields instead of the sea. I seem to remember that there was something like thirty locks, which we had to open and close without any assistance. It was tiring work made worse by the fact that our exhausts discharged from the side of the ship just below sea level. As a result, this splashed back onto us when we were tying up, so we had to pull on oilskins and sea boots every time we went through a lock. Another fault soon made apparent was that, due to the rocket blast screen, there was no view from the wheelhouse, consequently the helmsman was steering blind - that is to say, only by compass and orders from the bridge. This was not a particular disadvantage when at sea but, when one was going by way of the narrow canal, it was hopeless. However, the designers had evidently thought of this and the steering could be transferred up to the bridge meaning that the helmsman had to work from there. In spite of this, we twice ran aground onto the canal bank, fortunately whilst the coxswain was on the wheel, and we had to struggle back. This we managed quite easily the first time, but on the second time, someone had to swim the few yards to the opposite bank and fasten a line round the nearest tree, so that we could winch ourselves back into water. It was a good job that there were no sightseers, as we should never have lived it down. There were only a few sheep about and they didn't seem at all interested.

Loch Ness took up the bulk of the canal length. This was over twenty miles long and being on the helm was a joy as, being sheltered and with no wind, all that was needed was an occasional correction on the wheel every five minutes or so. This gave us a chance to enjoy the surrounding scenery, which I must say, was all quite spectacular. But Loch Ness itself was exceptional. The steeply banked sides of the loch were thickly covered by every variety of deciduous tree and being, by now, autumn they seemed to be every colour of the rainbow. My mother mentioned, when I saw her, that I had waxed lyrical about it all to her in my letters home. Many years later, whilst touring Scotland with my wife, Margaret, I made a detour and drove all round the loch to show her how grand things were. I was never more disappointed in my life to find that, by then, all the deciduous trees had been cut down and replaced with a drab covering of pine trees. I did read sometime after that, due to numerous complaints, they were reverting back to deciduous for which I, for one, was very pleased.

I might add that, although we kept a careful look out, we didn't catch any sight of the Loch Ness monster.

At the end of the loch was the small town of Fort Augustus and about half a dozen of us decided to blow in a lump of our hard-earned money and have dinner at the Lovatt Arms. This turned out to be a revelation as it was almost full of residents, mostly English, who had moved there to be far away from the war. These were some of the people for whom we had been fighting. To add insult to injury we realised that, although people were being served quite quickly, it appeared we were being ignored. One of the lads, who didn't give a damn for anybody, said that he would wake a few of them up, and promptly started eating the flowers on the table. These were tulips and he started eating them petal by petal with feigned enjoyment, although I bet they tasted awful. This evidently did not go un-noticed and in no time at all we were served with apologies for the delay, from the manager no less, as consciences had no doubt been stirred. All's well that ends well, but it did engender a sour note to our evening.

I think it took us several days to traverse the full length of the canal, but it was a unique experience which made all the little inconveniences we had experienced well worthwhile. On the journey, the first lieutenant managed to collect a shotgun and a ferret for rabbiting and I got the job of building a hutch (for the ferret, I mean, not the shotgun) and, being used to handling small stock, I soon found out that the little devils can't half bite. We became inundated for a few days with rabbits. Invariably, they had parts missing and were full of lead shot. He must have shot them at point blank distance. Nevertheless, they made a welcome addition to our meals. Rabbit was a popular meal in those days, but one hardly sees them nowadays, and then, I am given to understand, they come from China and are reared there and, moreover, are tasteless.

The end of the canal at last came at a little place called Corpach where we found, to our dismay, there was a continuous chain of, I think, eleven locks named Neptune's Staircase. It took us all the next day to negotiate them. It was hard work and we welcomed the visit to the local pub, where we were cheered by thrashing the locals at darts.

This took us out into Loch Linnhe, which was a sea loch, and then the open sea again. The scenery was again spectacular and the water was crystal clear. One could look down many feet, or I should say fathoms (there are six feet in a fathom). In fact, the water was so clear that I, personally, felt that we were not in a sea, but resting on a surface, like a transparent skin stretched above an abyss and, if that skin was broken, we would drop like a stone to smash ourselves on the bottom.

On our journey south from Scotland, while I was on duty one night, it was quite dark and, being a bit bored, I looked for something to do. We were trailing the ship's log behind us. This was made of heavy stainless steel about a foot long, almost like a torpedo, but with metal vanes at the end slightly twisted one way. The log was a sort of mileometer and at sea this was the only way there was of measuring speed and distance. There was a special mount on the guardrail and then a length of about fifty feet of log-line, which was special woven sennet line with the log fastened on the end. I pulled in the line and was absolutely astounded to see that the sea water that dripped off the line shone quite brightly with a vivid phosphorescent green bright light, moreover both my hand glowed with the same bright green glow. It was completely fascinating and I understand that it's caused when there is a concentration of bacteria or plankton in the sea. I had heard of it but was quite unprepared for what I saw. Looking forwards to the bows I could see that the bow-wave had the same green glow, I felt like waking everybody up to see it but decided that this would, perhaps, not be appreciated.

After Corpach, our next stop was Fort William where we stopped two or three days, and then on to Oban, another few days, and on to Troon. We were glad of the breaks, as boats like ours were never designed to be at sea for long periods. Being at sea was like being on the go twenty-four hours a day and, after a bit, we had had enough. We stopped at Troon for, if I can remember rightly, about two weeks, and got ashore quite a bit. It felt OK being ashore for a change. Two or three of us tried fishing in the harbour without much success, except for a few colefish, which weren't all that good to eat, but we also caught loads of eels of quite a decent size. The Londoners in our crew loved them fried in butter, but I was not tempted to try.

We were informed that our next destination was a place called Aberdovey in Wales where we would undergo intensive rocket firing trials. This would be comprised of loading up with dummy rockets and firing them onto the shore, which was the, apparently, well-known sands of Aberdovey. The best part was that the Army would then dig them up and replace them with flags, this was to work out the fall of shot pattern for our new ship. We were told that we should be inundated with all the back room 'boffins' and high-ranking officers. They would also construct a large steel box right up in the bows, which would house cameras and various other instruments. We were also asked if we would make an effort with our dress and be on our best behaviour.

Aberdovey was quite a nice little place and would, I suppose, have been a popular seaside resort, although none of us had ever heard of it. (Mind you, we had never heard of most of the small places we came to, and I can't remember what I've forgotten about any of them.) It had two wooden jetties and that was all, and, at one of them, there was a sailing ship belonging to The Outward Bound School. There were about a dozen or so young lads, that is to say younger than we, and a few of the more adventurous of them did come on board to have a look round and to have a good moan about the food and the discipline. We older people just smiled and commiserated with them, which I am sure (?) made them feel better.

We soon got to know our way around and became, to some extent, at loggerheads with the local lads as some of the crew were getting to know some of the local girls quite well. Another delightful thing was that the local milk-girl delivered a small churn of fresh milk every morning. Fresh milk. I haven't mentioned that food-wise, although we lived extremely well, we never got any fresh milk and had to manage with Carnation evaporated milk which, although you could get used to it after a time, was no substitute for the real thing.

Whilst at Aberdovey we were asked if we could supply any lads to play in the local football team and they finished up with five of us; they, apparently, were always short of a full team. I, like a fool, let myself get roped in. I forget who we were playing against, but it was in the East Cambrian Coast league. We were defeated ignominiously, one reason being that, although we were all pretty fit, the difference between doing acrobatics with the hammock bars in the rocket magazine and, say, distance running soon showed up. After running up and down the football pitch we were absolutely shattered. We weren't asked again.

They are a funny lot, the Welsh. It was not unusual to find that, when a few of us went into the local pub, the regulars who had been speaking English, immediately lapsed into Welsh. As we got on quite well otherwise, it was a bit disconcerting at least. Perhaps we had all got B.O. and nobody had told us.

The new crew soon got to know each other and got on well enough. There was one particular lad, a proper cockney from The Elephant and Castle, who cottoned on to me. He was a nice lad, although not that 'bright', and I was surprised when, one day, evidently very embarrassed, asked me if I would address the envelopes for him when he wrote home to his mother, as only she was able to read his atrocious writing.

This same lad, apparently, was quite scared about when we were going to fire the rockets. Apparently, some of the lads had been 'having him on' about how terrifying it was. When the time actually came and we were coming into the beach, somebody said that the hatch cover up in front of the rockets had not been closed. This lad immediately said he would do it and dashed off forrard. He came back after a few minutes with a handkerchief wrapped round his hand, soaked in blood. In his panic he had taken off the latch holding the hatch cover in place and it had dropped down. It probably weighed something like half a hundredweight and it had dropped onto his thumb chopping it off at the first joint. Our first casualty and one for which we felt very guilty, especially the person who had mentioned the closed hatch and let the lad do the job. There is no place on board a ship for playing practical jokes.

There was another lad, part of our original crew who, it turned out soon after we got together, was a homosexual. He was a likeable person, very intelligent, and got on well with everybody. Apparently, he had been at Art College at Newcastle before he had been called up, and both his parents were working in the Persian Gulf and made him a generous allowance. He assimilated well into the crew but, as you can imagine, he came in for an awful amount of ragging, some of which made even me blush. On one occasion, one lad asked him when it was that he first found out that he was a 'puff'. His immediate reply, given without a second's hesitation, was 'at the age of three when I accidentally sat on a dummy'. I think that that reply, which resulted in much laughter, won him the day and thereafter he was just accepted and nobody ever said any more.

Again, the time came for us to move on. Apparently, all being well, our next stop would be Dartmouth in Devon. That was, if everything went as expected. It was a bit like the 'Round Britain Race', except that we weren't going to win any prizes. Everything went well and we arrived in the late afternoon. I rather liked Dartmouth and, many years later, my wife and I spent two or three holidays there.

It was funny that, at the small guest house where we stayed during the first holiday, the lady ran the hotel and her husband was a fisherman and owned his own crab boat. He was a quiet person, but drawing him out a little, talking about crabbing and lobster fishing, I told him I had been in the navy on small ships. A day or two later he asked me if I would like to a day out with him. I said yes please, and it was all arranged, with a very early start the next morning. That night at dinner, his wife said that she understood that I was going out with him the next day. I was quite pleased with what she said next. She asked me what it was that I'd got. I asked what she meant and she replied that many visitors had asked if it was possible to go out with him, but he had never obliged, and 'you didn't even ask him'. I remarked that we were evidently birds of a feather.

We set out next morning and he immediately asked if I would take over the boat whilst he got on with cutting up some bait for the lobster pots. He pointed out roughly where we where and where we were going and just left everything to me. Fortunately, there was not much traffic in the harbour so I didn't make a mess of things and after about three quarters of an hour, he told me to make for a gap between two lots of rocks. I was a bit apprehensive of being in charge of such a very expensive boat, but he seemed quite happy with the way I was performing. He started reeling in the lobster pots and told me to keep clear as he had seen more than one instance of a fisherman losing a finger with the line travelling on the electric winch. We had a good catch and, eventually, he said for me to take the boat back whilst he sorted out the catch of crabs and lobsters. I was thoroughly enjoying myself, the weather was beautiful and I was, by now, more relaxed and life was good. We got back to the harbour which was, by then, quite busy and I had to thread my way round other boats, dinghies and bigger stuff. I said that perhaps he ought to take over now. He did and, rather amused, remarked that he was waiting to see when I would say that. It was nothing really but I have always remembered every minute of that trip. The perfect day finished when I saw his wife who had arranged for my wife and I to have a lobster salad for dinner. She said that her husband had been given a salmon, which a pal of his had caught the previous day, and, if it was all right with us, she was going to do us a salmon salad, but with a lobster starter. Was that all right? I nipped out and a got a bottle of wine and we dined like royalty that evening. She said that most of her visitors didn't particularly like fish and neither did she or her family.

However, to carry on with the main story, we only stopped at Dartmouth one day and off we went. Next stop Southampton. It took a couple of days and back we were. We tied up at part of the old docks where we had not been before. It was like a ships' graveyard as most of them had no crew and were just stacked up there. It was a bit sad really.

When we'd been some time at Southampton, the flotilla skipper decided that we should hold a flotilla sports day. This would consist of swimming, rowing, figure of eight sculling, that is with one oar over the stern of the boat, and one or two races consisting of some combination of these. I assumed, quite wrongly as it happened, that I would be a 'cert' for the 'heaving line throwing', and just stood there holding my heaving line stupidly. Nobody particularly shone at this, and a couple of our lads shouted at me to have a go and show how it should be done. Being big headed, I stood forward and had a go and on the first, and only, throw my line went a good ten feet further than any other. The officer who was keeping the marks asked me for my name and, when I told him, replied that my name was not on the list and asked why not? It seems that the first lieutenant had been asked to supply a list of names for the event and to try to enter a couple of names for each race. Usually, in such cases, the crew supplied the names, as they knew who was the best at what. In our case, however, the officer had used his own judgement, which was, perhaps, not the best way.

And there, I thought, the matter finished. Later, however, our first lieutenant tackled me and accused me of trying to make him look him a fool. I was so incensed that I nearly replied that it didn't need me to do that. Fortunately, common sense prevailed and I replied that that had not been my intention and, if he had taken it that way, I could only apologise. There is no harm in lying occasionally.

The only thing that we won that day was the figure of eight sculling, as one of our lads was a natural and it was not easy. The fact was, while we had been stopped at Troon, we had spent all day fetching and loading stores. Usually two were sent to go for the foodstuffs et cetera, but in this case our 'Jimmy' said that only one could be spared. We were 'at it' all day, as we had to take on water, diesel oil and coal for the galley stove. It got to about five o'clock and 'the Owl', as one of our crew was nicknamed, had still not got back, but then a boat appeared on the far side of the dock and there he was. He had got, as well as all the other stuff, three bags of potatoes, vegetables and a couple of sacks of bread, and there he was perched on top of it all, sculling over the stern. It was a good job he was good at it as there was no room to sit and use both oars. This lad was always in trouble. Once, as he was on quartermaster duty, he was walking along the deck, wearing the usual white belt and gaiters and reading a paperback. He was so involved in the book that he didn't notice the usual bit of guard-rail missing and walked straight overboard in to the sea. On another occasion, I caught him in the engine room. There was a large fuse box holding about twenty pairs of fuses and he was running two fingers down the pairs of fuses to test which one had blown. I was amazed, but it seemed that he had a natural very dry skin and all he felt was a tingle. I gave him a right rollocking, as I had already caught him lighting a cigarette by partly opening one of the main switches on the main switchboard until it arched across. It was an absolutely stupid thing to do, but that was 'the Owl'.

It was not unusual, especially if you had a piano, when sitting around in the evening, for someone to break into singing one of the popular songs, or a hymn, with everyone soon joining in. Both myself and one of the other lads had been in church choirs and I distinctly remember, on one occasion, we all sang 'Abide with me' with two different descants and, although I say it myself, it sounded pretty good.

We just kicked our heels in Southampton for what seemed ages but gradually, one by one, some of the crew got there demob papers and we said goodbye. We knew that we would probably never see each other again and it was a bit sad.

About half of the crew disappeared, including Lofty, and a volunteer was called for to take over the duties of cook. To my surprise, my pal, who had been an apprenticed pastry-cook at home, said that he would do it, provided that I joined him. It was rather a good idea, really, as it meant that shore leave at night still left somebody to cook the evening meal. Moreover, I had always been interested in cooking. Some would say 'Jack of all trades', forgetting the second part of that particular saying.

This went on for some time, though I can't remember how long, and I began to worry as to when

I would get my papers. On enquiring, I was told that I could not go until a replacement had been found, and qualified men were not thick on the ground. I remember one evening, a few of us were still playing cards after the generator had been switched off. We were using the emergency lighting and were well supplied from our illicit stock of rum. It got around to talking about our past experiences, and as the old naval saying goes, 'the lamp was swinging well'.

I had already come across our old ship L.C.T 363 and was telling about what gory happenings had taken place, including the rumour about when it had been just a Tank Landing Craft. This was that an Ordinary Seaman had once hung himself in the starboard locker. I don't know how much truth there was in it, but it made a good story. I don't know whether it is the sea, but most sailors get to be a bit superstitious and, after a while, nobody seemed to want to go up top to have a wee over the side unless somebody went with him.

In time, my turn to leave came and, after getting together all my kit, I was off, after saying my goodbyes all round. Apparently there was a special train which, I think, started at Southampton. I should say that the whole of the Navy Combined Operations was not based at one of the usual naval bases, but was under their own base named HMS Copra, which was at a place named Rosneath on Gare Loch. This train was to travel north to Glasgow, then on to Greenock and then, by ferry, across the Firth of Clyde. I think it took us a couple of days and we were supplied with packed lunches and tea. No rum!

The camp was a huge place consisting of Nissan huts and in a pine forest. It had been an American camp and, by then, was fairly dilapidated, in fact quite a dump, but after, I think, three days, I was given my discharge papers and a railway ticket back to Sheffield, after handing over most of my kit. Also, I had to collect my 'demob' suit at York. Somewhat dejected, I was on my way home, after getting my new clothes at York, including a trilby hat, which I never wore. I, eventually, got back home feeling a bit lost. I don't know which was the worst, joining the navy, or leaving it.

That was it, I was now a civilian like it or not and I had to find my way back into the world. But that is an entirely different story. All I had to remind me was a sailmaker's palm, a bosun's pipe and a little cardboard box containing five medals and ribbons, not worn.